*The Cambridge Introduction to*
## Zora Neale Hurston

*Their Eyes Were Watching God* is a key text in African American
literature. Its author Zora Neale Hurston has become an iconic figure for
her literary works and for her invaluable contribution to documenting
elements of black folk culture in the rural south and in the Caribbean.
This introductory book designed for students explores Hurston's artistic
achievements and her unique character: her staunch individualism, her
penchant for drama, her sometimes controversial politics, her
philosophical influences and her views on gender relations. Lovalerie
King explores Hurston's life and analyzes her major works and short
stories. Historical, social, political, and cultural contexts for Hurston's
life and work, including her key role in the development of the Harlem
Renaissance, are set out. The book concludes with an overview of the
reception of Hurston's work, both in her lifetime and up to the present,
as well as suggestions for further reading.

Lovalerie King is Assistant Professor of African American Literature
at Pennsylvania State University.

# The Cambridge Introduction to
# Zora Neale Hurston

LOVALERIE KING

CAMBRIDGE
UNIVERSITY PRESS

CAMBRIDGE UNIVERSITY PRESS
Cambridge, New York, Melbourne, Madrid, Cape Town, Singapore, São Paulo, Delhi

Cambridge University Press
The Edinburgh Building, Cambridge CB2 8RU, UK

Published in the United States of America by Cambridge University Press, New York

www.cambridge.org
Information on this title: www.cambridge.org/9780521670951

First published 2008

Printed in the United Kingdom at the University Press, Cambridge

*A catalogue record for this publication is available from the British Library*

*Library of Congress Cataloguing in Publication data*
King, Lovalerie.
The Cambridge introduction to Zora Neale Hurston / Lovalerie King.
   p.   cm.
Includes bibliographical references and index.
ISBN 978-0-521-85457-3
1. Hurston, Zora Neale – Criticism and interpretation.    I. Title.
PS3515.U789Z763   2008
813'.52 – dc22      2008025896

ISBN 978-0-521-85457-3 hardback
ISBN 978-0-521-67095-1 paperback

*For My Baby Sister*
*Earnestine (Tiny) Cassandra King*

# Contents

# Preface

This volume introduces Hurston and her works in a manner that makes evident her full engagement with life and her continuing significance to African American women's literature, African American literature, American history and literature, cultural anthropology, and gender studies. She is one of very few African American women writers whose work most college students will experience during her or his undergraduate career. In the tradition of African American women writers, her name is as familiar as that of Toni Morrison and Alice Walker; yet she died in relative obscurity – a staunch individualist to the very end. Since Alice Walker and others rescued Hurston from literary oblivion in the 1970s, several scholars have produced works focusing on her life, work, philosophy, politics, and critical reception.[1]

This volume, intended for general readers, is divided into four sections: Life, Contexts, Works, and Critical Reception. The chapter on Hurston's life places the author in her historical, social, and political milieu. Beginning with her early life as a precocious child in the all-black town of Eatonville, Florida, the chapter charts Hurston's intimate relationships, educational experiences, participation in the Harlem Renaissance/New Negro Movement, post-Renaissance activities and, finally, decline, death, and cultural resurrection. It examines significant life-shaping events and experiences, such as her premature exit from home following her mother's death and her father's remarriage, her arrival in Harlem just as the New Negro Movement was heating up, her marriages, the love affair of her life with Percival Punter, studying with famed anthropologist Franz Boas, her (sometimes problematic) association with patron Charlotte Osgood Mason, the never-ending struggle to secure financing for her literary endeavors, and her travels and fieldwork.

Long before she became a trained anthropologist, Hurston drew on her capacities for entertaining and storytelling to weather some difficult adolescent and early adult years. Later, her particular genius revealed itself in the ability to combine skills acquired during formal education and fieldwork with her natural talent for storytelling and performance. Chapter 1 also provides information about Hurston's strong tendencies toward drama and the dramatic, even as the formal development of her skills in that arena often took a backseat to other demands on her creative energies for several reasons, including the strong individualist spirit that undermined collaborative endeavors. Finally, the chapter sheds light on Hurston's place in the "historiography" of black womanist/feminist thought and action. Thus, the information in chapter one presents Hurston as a multi-faceted woman living her "several lives" (as much as possible) on her own terms. Overall, readers should obtain from this chapter a general understanding of the highs and lows of Hurston's life and literary career.

Chapter 2 considers historical, social, political, and cultural contexts for Hurston's life and literary production. Hurston came of age during a period that has come to be known as the *nadir* for African Americans in terms of economic and political progress; yet, Hurston recalls her youth (until the age of thirteen) in insular Eatonville, Florida, as a happy time of relative prosperity. The chapter begins with a look at some of the events and circumstances occurring during the decades preceding Hurston's birth, including the Civil War, the abolishment of slavery, Radical Reconstruction, and the rise of white supremacist terror groups. It continues with some consideration of Jim Crow segregation in the late nineteenth century along with a generally regressive political climate in terms of rights and privileges for African Americans. The chapter also recounts African America's collective and individual responses to the increasingly hostile social and political climate. It calls attention to competing ideologies and discourses of womanhood that influenced Hurston's explorations of black female sexuality and her focus on gender relations throughout her fiction. Politically conservative, Hurston often wrote against the grain and suffered the negative criticism of her contemporaries as a result; the choices she made in her professional life reflect the independent spirit that was evident from early childhood.

Chapter 3 introduces readers to Hurston's substantial body of published fiction; the objective here is to show, among other things, how Hurston's work celebrates – at an organic level – the tradition of African American literature that began with oral forms brought from Africa to the New World. Note is taken of the fact that Hurston's production was outstanding during that period, particularly because she was neither white, nor male, nor affluent; she published seven books and scores of essays, short stories, and plays between the 1920s and the time of her death in 1960. The chapter also notes posthumously published and variously edited volumes of her work, though Hurston's best-known and most widely taught work, *Their Eyes Were Watching God*, serves as the centerpiece. Readers are treated to several vantage points from which to experience the novel and to understand its relevance to several academic fields and disciplines.

Discussions of Hurston's shorter works highlight recurring themes and issues, with special attention to some of her most often anthologized short stories. Overall, the chapter assists in a better understanding of Hurston's works at the level of plot, character, narrative, and structure.

The fourth chapter, "Critical Reception," provides readers with an overview of factors influencing how Hurston's work has been read and understood both during her life and since her death, with the bulk of the chapter focusing on the latter period. Hurston's somewhat mixed (and often hostile) early reception has been a recurring issue in scholarship on her life and work; contemporaneous reviews often diverged along racial and/or political lines. Other factors, such as target audience demographics, and the patronage upon which a number of authors relied played a role in what was published and how it was received. While the same factors continue to influence literary production, contemporary criticism of Hurston's work tends to focus much more on her artistry and on the ways that her body of work appeals to a variety of area studies and disciplines, including English and Literary Studies, African American Studies, Gender Studies, Anthropology, and History. While the chapter's primary objective is to survey a variety of critical perspectives on Hurston's work, it also provides analysis that helps readers understand how context and the development of literary and critical studies have contributed to the vast difference between her contemporaneous and contemporary receptions. The hope is that readers will emerge with a stronger appreciation for the role historical context plays in the forms and nature that literature and criticism take, and also with a full appreciation of Hurston's unique and valuable contributions to American literature and culture. A list of suggested readings for further study rounds out this volume on one of the world's major wordsmiths.

## Note

1. These include, for example, Robert E. Hemenway, *Zora Neale Hurston: A Literary Biography* (Chicago and Urbana, IL: University of Illinois Press, 1977, 1980); N. Y. Nathiri, *Zora!: Zora Neale Hurston, A Woman and Her Community* (Orlando, FA: The Orlando Sentinel, 1991); Ayana L. Karanja, *Zora Neale Hurston: The Breath of Her Voice* (New York: Peter Lang, 1999); Valerie Boyd, *Wrapped in Rainbows: The Life of Zora Neale Hurston* (New York: Scribner's, 2003); Deborah G. Plant, *Every Tub Must Sit on Its Own Bottom* (Urbana, IL and Chicago: University of Illinois Press, 1995); and Carla Kaplan, ed., *Zora Neale Hurston: A Life in Letters* (New York: Doubleday, 2002).

## Acknowledgments

I would like to acknowledge recommendations, feedback, and/or moral support from the following wonderful human beings: MaryEmma Graham at the University of Kansas, Trudier Harris at the University of North Carolina at Chapel Hill, and all my other Wintergreen sisters. I would like to thank my editor Ray Ryan for taking a chance on an Assistant Professor, and my friends and colleagues Su Fang Ng and Carla Mulford for reading my drafts and offering their comments kindly. Hugs and kisses to my daughter Erin King, the one person in the whole world who *gets me* 100 percent of the time. Thanks also to Bruce Allen Hughes, the volume indexer, and so much more.

## Abbreviations

| | |
|---|---|
| DTOAR | *Dust Tracks on a Road* |
| JGV | *Jonah's Gourd Vine* |
| MMOTM | *Moses, Man of the Mountain* |
| MAM | *Mules and Men* |
| SOTS | *Seraph on the Suwanee* |
| TMH | *Tell My Horse* |
| TEWWG | *Their Eyes Were Watching God* |

# Chapter 1

# Life

Born under the sign of Capricorn on January 7, 1891 in Notasulga, Alabama, Zora Neale Hurston was the sixth child and second daughter of John Hurston (1861–1918) and Lucy Ann Potts Hurston (1865–1904). Hurston's biographers tell us that her name was recorded in the family bible as Zora Neal Lee Hurston; at some point an "e" was added to "Neal" and "Lee" was dropped. Though she was born in Notasulga, Hurston always called Eatonville, Florida, home and even – though perhaps unwittingly, because her family relocated to Eatonville when Zora was quite young – named it as her birthplace in her autobiography. Eatonville has become famous for its long association with Hurston; since 1991 it has been the site of the annual multi-disciplinary Zora Neale Hurston Festival of the Arts and Humanities (ZORA! Festival), which lasts for several days. The festival's broad objective is to call attention to contributions that Africa-derived persons have made to world culture; however, its narrower objective is to celebrate Hurston's life and work along with Eatonville's unique cultural history.

Hurston's family moved to Eatonville in 1893. Her father, John Hurston, was the eldest of nine children in an impoverished sharecropper family near Notasulga; during his lifetime, he would achieve substantial influence in and around Eatonville as a minister, carpenter, successful family man, and local politician. His parents, Alfred and Amy Hurston, were, like wife Lucy's parents, Sarah and Richard Potts, formerly enslaved persons. According to Hurston and her biographers, the landowning Potts family looked down on the hand-to-mouth sharecropping Hurstons who lived across the creek.[1] By the time John spotted 14-year-old Lucy singing in her church choir, the class distinction between the landowning Potts family and the sharecropping Hurston family was well known; indeed, Potts family resistance to the marriage offers an interesting study in African American class dynamics of the time. Neither of Lucy's parents wanted her to marry John Hurston, who was – in addition to being dirt poor – rumored to be the bastard son of a white man; Hurston's biographer, Valerie Boyd, has suggested that John possibly owed his light skin to the fact that father Alfred was mulatto. Disdainful of Lucy's choice, Sarah Potts refused to attend Lucy and John's wedding and barred her daughter from her childhood home.

John Hurston, a man imbued with not a small amount of wanderlust, first visited Eatonville, Florida, around 1890. By the time the family moved there in 1893, Lucy had given him six children. The oldest child was Hezekiah Robert (shortened to Bob), born November 1882. Isaac (1883), born after Bob, died very young. John Cornelius (1885), Richard William (1887), Sarah Emmeline (1889), and Zora (1891) followed. After the family moved to Eatonville, Lucy gave birth to Clifford Joel (1893), Benjamin Franklin (1895), and Everett Edward (1898). In Eatonville, the family prospered far beyond their humble roots in Notasulga, Alabama. No doubt, the same strength of character that led Lucy to defy her parents and marry the man of her choice also served her during the very lean early years of the marriage and her husband's many infidelities. She emerges in works about Hurston's life as the center of the Hurston household, the pillar of strength that served to shape her children's character and direct her husband toward his professional potential. John Hurston possessed substantial carpentry skills. After he moved to Eatonville, he became a minister and, ultimately, served three terms as Eatonville's mayor, authoring many of its laws. A former teacher, Lucy Potts Hurston routinely helped her young children with their schoolwork, making education a central aspect of their upbringing. She urged them to "jump at the sun," and she especially encouraged young Zora's creative impulses.

Zora excelled in the language arts and, early on, exhibited her talent as a storyteller and performer. While Lucy Potts Hurston applauded and (for the most part) encouraged the development of her daughter's vibrant individuality, John Hurston did not. Indeed, he and Zora were usually at odds with each other. According to Hurston and her biographers, John Hurston had welcomed one daughter, but saw having two as more of a liability than he was willing to take on. Zora was a female whose natural way of behaving in the world challenged and undermined gender role expectations; in addition she was strong-willed and often at odds with authority. Outgoing and tough, she could punch as hard as the boys with whom she played and fought. Despite the fact that Zora and her father seemed destined to be at odds from the day she was born a female rather than a male, she actually had much in common with John Hurston, including her capacity for hard work combined with a wanderlust and desire to seek out the horizon.

Hurston's home life changed dramatically after her mother died on September 18, 1904 and 44-year-old John Hurston remarried on February 12, 1905. The home that had been a nurturing and comparatively safe haven for the Hurston siblings became decidedly less so. Indeed, it became a site of conflict once second wife, twenty-year-old Mattie Moge, took her place in the household. The marriage, so soon after Lucy Hurston's death, met with the resentment of the Hurston siblings and the black community of Eatonville. According to Zora, the household soon began to fall apart. John's favorite daughter, Sarah, married quickly and moved away, taking young Everett with her.

John Hurston had sent Zora away to attend school at Florida Baptist Academy in Jacksonville, Florida, immediately following her mother's death. With her natural bookishness and her exuberant spirit, Zora fared well during her year at Florida Baptist Academy – though her arrival in Jacksonville meant being cast against an unwelcoming white backdrop. One of the central objectives for faculty and administrators at Florida Baptist Academy was to teach its charges about their proper place in American society. For someone like Hurston, such conditioning was almost impossible. Still the white backdrop in Jacksonville signified her difference, that she was colored and therefore not standard.

At the end of the school year, Zora found herself *abandoned* when her father (who had failed to pay her room and board) refused to send money for her trip home. A school administrator advanced Zora the fare and, back in Eatonville, she observed the neglectful way that her father and stepmother regarded her younger siblings. The older children were being driven away one after another as John Hurston buckled under his own weaknesses and the will of his young second wife. As might be expected, Zora was soon at odds with Mattie Moge, and she left her family home later in 1905 feeling "orphaned and lonesome."[2] Had she been male, her father might simply have borne the expense of schooling as he did for his sons.

Hurston wrote of this time that she was "shifted from house to house of relatives and friends and found comfort nowhere."[3] Schooling was irregular and she missed her books. She recalled that she had actually foreseen her homelessness in one of a series of prescient visions she began having when she was 7. By the time Hurston was 15, she was working intermittently serving as home care nurse to elderly whites, or serving in a purely domestic capacity to others. Her autobiography provides interesting details about some of her experiences during this period, including being fired from one plum babysitting job because the older black housekeeper saw her as a threat, and losing another position after making the mistake of telling the woman of the house about her husband's unwelcome advances. Essentially, she failed at housekeeping jobs because she was simply not the subservient type and because she was more interested in her employers' books than in cleaning their homes.

In 1911 Hurston returned to the family home briefly and quickly found the situation unbearable. After a physical confrontation with her stepmother, she left again to look for work in a nearby town. She recalls finding a copy of Milton's *Paradise Lost* (1667) in a pile of rubbish and reading it because she "liked it," luxuriating in "Milton's syllables and rhythms without ever having heard that Milton was one of the greatest poets of the world."[4] Looking for work took on secondary importance to reading and understanding Milton; nevertheless, she soon found a temporary and somewhat satisfying job at a doctor's office that might have turned into a permanent position had oldest brother Hezekiah Robert not lured her with the promise of further schooling to come and live with his family.

Thrilled at the thought of living among relatives again – with the promise of further schooling – Hurston left her job and went to live with her brother, his wife, and their children; the family relocated to Memphis, Tennessee, in 1913. After three years of unpaid housework and babysitting, with no schooling on the horizon, Hurston moved on to her next adventure. Valerie Boyd points out in *Wrapped in Rainbows* that though Hurston wrote in *Dust Tracks on a Road* that she left her brother Bob's house in Memphis to take a position as a lady's maid with a theatrical group, that job actually came after she had lived with brother John and his wife Blanche in Jacksonville and subsequently endured a painful personal common-law relationship with someone she loved deeply but who treated her horribly, an experience she foresaw in one of her childhood visions.[5] We can attribute much of the silence surrounding this relationship to Hurston's desire to keep her most intimate matters away from the prying eyes of the world.

Hurston's next life-changing experience included her service as lady's maid to the lead singer of a Gilbert and Sullivan troupe. The position promised a good salary but, more important, it helped her to develop a degree of sophistication about the world. Her employer, of whom Hurston became very fond, even paid for a manicure course; the training would later serve Hurston well while she attended Howard University in Washington, DC. Most importantly, her time with the Gilbert and Sullivan troupe satisfied (at least temporarily) the wanderlust she had inherited from her father, John. During the time that Hurston lived away from her family home, her father was elected to three terms as Eatonville's mayor. In 1918, he died in Memphis after his car was struck by a train. Hurston did not attend the funeral. Traveling with the troupe, she lived among a diverse group of human beings, read books borrowed from a Harvard-trained troupe member, and acquired knowledge about music and theatrical production. A natural born performer, Hurston reveled in this atmosphere. She recalled the period as generally good, as a time when she learned about negotiating space for herself, and when she developed survival strategies for the times ahead. By the time her stint with the company ended in 1917 in Baltimore, Maryland, she had traveled extensively; however, she longed for more formal education and resolved to return to school.

In Baltimore, Hurston lied about her date of birth to qualify for free schooling, and this accounts in part for early discrepancies about her actual date of birth. She simply told officials she had been born ten years later and became sixteen again. Taking a job as a waitress, she first attended school at night. Later, she enrolled at the elite Morgan Academy, the high-school division of what would become Morgan State University. Hurston's entrance examination scores revealed her promise as a scholar, and good fortune shone on her, for the school's dean helped her secure work that allowed her to attend the academy. Hurston performed well in everything except mathematics, while interacting with classmates from Baltimore's "best" black families. Her lucky stars continued to shine at Morgan because it was there that she met a visiting Howard University student named May Miller, who suggested that she try her luck at Howard, another historically black institution of higher education. The daughter of a Howard sociologist, Miller went on to become a well-known playwright and poet. Following her suggestion and her Morgan friends' prodding, Hurston moved to Washington, found a job as a waitress, and settled down to earn money to pay her college expenses. In the interim, she enrolled in preparatory courses at Howard Academy.

At Howard University, she would meet a number of influential persons, perhaps chief among them philosophy professor Alain Locke, who would edit the collection whose title became synonymous with the Harlem Renaissance: *The New Negro* (1925).[6] Hurston wrote bad poetry, joined the Zeta Phi Beta sorority, and met fellow student Herbert Sheen, the man who became her first husband some years later. She also joined the staff of Howard's literary club journal, *The Stylus*, where her first published short story, the somewhat autobiographical "John Redding Goes to Sea," appeared in May 1921.[7] In addition, Hurston's affiliation with *Stylus* permitted her to attend poet Georgia Douglas Johnson's famous literary salons and rub elbows with poets, playwrights, novelists, and critics who have since become associated with the Harlem Renaissance / New Negro Movement. Though Hurston never completed the four-year degree program at Howard, her presence there in the early 1920s resulted in Alain Locke's bringing Hurston's promise as a writer to the attention of Charles S. Johnson, editor of *Opportunity Magazine*.

Upon Johnson's invitation, Hurston submitted "Drenched in Light" to *Opportunity*.[8] The short story, which was even more autobiographical than "John Redding Goes to Sea," appeared in the December 1924 issue. The next month, as she turned 34, Hurston moved to New York City. Her timing could not have been better because 1925 ended as a banner year for the budding author and other artists associated with the New Negro Movement. On May 1, 1925, she won two cash prizes and two honorable mentions at the *Opportunity* literary contest awards dinner. She also met and formed fruitful associations with three influential white Americans at that dinner. The first of these was Annie Nathan Meyer (1867–1951), a prolific author and a founder of Barnard College, who offered Hurston a chance to attend the college beginning in the fall of 1925. As Barnard's only black student, Hurston would eventually come under the influence and mentorship of eminent Columbia University anthropologist Franz Boas (1858–1942). Through her association with Boas, she began her groundbreaking research in southern and (ultimately) Caribbean folk culture that would culminate in *Mules and Men* and *Tell My Horse*.[9] She also met Fannie Hurst (1889–1968), a prolific novelist and short-story writer, whose list of publications ultimately spanned five full decades. Hurston served a brief time as Hurst's personal secretary, actually living with her for a month. The position allowed Hurston the flexible work schedule she needed in order to focus on her Barnard studies, but Hurst soon fired Hurston and the two became traveling companions and developed an interesting relationship that was friendly but not exactly a friendship. Rounding out the trio of influential people Hurston met at the May 1, 1925 *Opportunity* dinner was the well-connected Carl Van Vechten (1880–1964), a journalist, photographer, author, and patron of the Harlem Renaissance.

Two months after the *Opportunity* awards dinner, the *Spokesman* published Hurston's short story, "Magnolia Flower," and in September *The Messenger* published her essay "The Hue and Cry about Howard University." Hurston's coming-out year culminated in the November release of Alain Locke's *The New Negro*, which included her short story "Spunk" along with works by Jean Toomer, Bruce Nugent, Claude McKay, Countee Cullen, Langston Hughes, Georgia Douglas Johnson, Anne Spencer, Angelina Grimke, and other authors whose names would become associated with the New Negro Movement. Hurston had indeed *arrived*. Finally, in December, she published "Under the Bridge" – a short story whose themes she would repeat in "Sweat" (1926) – in *The X-Ray: The Official Publication of Zeta Phi Beta Sorority*. While she attended classes at Barnard, she joined Hughes, Wallace Thurman and several other younger artists in the publication of the short-lived *FIRE!!*, a literary journal that saw only one issue, in November 1926, and to which Hurston contributed a revised version of her play, "Color Struck," and the short story, "Sweat."[10]

The Harlem Renaissance thus served as the backdrop for a number of Hurston's early achievements in fiction, drama, and poetry, while it was actually during the decade following the 1929 Stock market Crash (which brought on the Great Depression) that she would publish five of her seven longer works: *Jonah's Gourd Vine* (1934); *Mules and Men* (1935); *Their Eyes Were Watching God* (1937); *Tell My Horse* (1938); and *Moses, Man of the Mountain* (1939). She produced almost all of her work against the backdrop of Jim Crow segregation and the concomitant racialized social and political issues that prevailed in America during her life. She was highly productive during her travels, producing *Their Eyes Were Watching God* while studying religion and folklore in the Caribbean and collecting materials for *Tell My Horse*. Her work on African religious practices detailed in *Tell My Horse* provides insight into the politics, sociology, and anthropology of Haiti and Jamaica and also (along with *Mules and Men* and her work with the Florida Writers' Project) serves as important source material for her works of fiction.

In 1927, with a research fellowship arranged by Franz Boas, Hurston traveled south to collect folk songs and folk tales. In *Dust Tracks on a Road*, she characterizes research as "formalized curiosity," as "poking and prying with a purpose."[11] She used part of her first formal research period to reconnect with family members and to marry Herbert Sheen on May 19, 1927 in St. Augustine, Florida. Her affair with Sheen had continued from their Howard years together – the affair lasting longer than the marriage, which ended in divorce in July 1931. Sheen, a medical student in Chicago, Illinois, at the time of the wedding, returned to his studies only a few days after the ceremony, and Hurston turned again to her travels through the south. Near Mobile, Alabama, she interviewed Cudjo Lewis, who was then believed to be the last surviving member of a group of Africans from the last slave ship to land in the United States. Langston Hughes traveled with Hurston through the south during part of the summer of 1927, and they became closer friends. Occasionally, they stopped to lecture at schools along the way.

Hurston recalled in her autobiography that her first attempts to collect folk tales and folk songs among people with whom she should have been very familiar were not particularly fruitful. The sophistication she had acquired and learned to exude in the north only served to distance her from her richest potential sources of information: rural black southerners. The result was a disappointing research experience. She fared much better during subsequent trips when she realized that people would be more forthcoming if she gained their trust by becoming part of the community, an insider. The approach became the hallmark of her subsequent research experiences, but it occasionally placed her in life-threatening situations – including one incident described in *Mules and Men* when she narrowly avoided being knifed by a jealous woman.

Like her fellow artists, Hurston needed two things in order to produce her work: a means of support and time to work. During her travels with Langston

Hughes in the summer of 1927, Hughes shared information with Hurston about Charlotte Osgood Mason (1854–1946), a wealthy widow and patron of the arts who lived at 399 Park Avenue in Manhattan. Alain Locke served at the time as Mason's paid adviser on matters related to Negro art and artists. An introduction was arranged, and Hurston first met Mason – who insisted that her beneficiaries call her Godmother – on September 20, 1927. The two signed a contract in December 1927. In her seventies at the time, Mason would support Hurston's research and writing for several years to come. Her initial investment was $200 a month for a two-year period, along with an automobile and a motion-picture camera. Essentially, the contract between the two women meant that Hurston would collect materials that could only be published with Mason's consent. Mason would later attempt to assert her authority over all of Hurston's work. While Hurston tried in her autobiography to put the best face on what now seems like her indentured status, the amount of control Mason exerted over Hurston has been well documented in Hurston's biographies and collected letters. Regardless, when 36-year-old Hurston returned south in December 1927, she had developed a methodology for collecting the folk tales and songs that would ultimately serve as the source material for *Mules and Men.*

Meanwhile, she continued to publish in a variety of venues and to maintain her status as a member of the black literary world. In October 1927, along with her first piece on Cudjo Lewis, she had published an article about a black settlement at St. Augustine, Florida, in the *Journal of Negro History.*[12] The following year in May, she published the often-anthologized essay, "How It Feels to Be Colored Me," in *The World Tomorrow.* Wallace Thurman satirized her as Sweetie Mae Carr in *Infants of the Spring* (1928) – a satirical novel about the black literati in Harlem – and that same year she received her BA from Barnard. Between 1930 and 1932, she worked at organizing her research notes for *Mules and Men.* In 1931 and 1933, respectively, she published "Hoodoo in America" in the *Journal of American Folklore* and "The Gilded Six-Bits" in *Story.* Hurston had a stellar year in 1934: she contributed six essays to Nancy Cunard's anthology, *Negro,* and published both *Jonah's Gourd Vine* (based on the relationship between her mother and father) and "The Fire and the Cloud" (the seed story for *Moses, Man of the Mountain*) in *Challenge.*[13]

Hurston also had her first formal theater experiences during the early 1930s. Valerie Boyd's characterization of Hurston as having been bitten by the theater bug around that time is an understatement considering the fact that Hurston demonstrated a predilection for drama and performance from the time of her childhood; even her birth was unusually dramatic, having come at a time when the only available "midwife" was a white male neighbor who happened to stop by the house where her mother was alone and in the throes of labor. Hurston made her way out of the womb unassisted, and some months later she took her first steps on her own after sensing a threat from a pig that had entered the house. Equally inclined toward performance art as a young girl, she constructed miniature figures from the materials available to her and helped them to perform as characters in stories she made up about them. Hurston has also detailed in several writings, including her autobiography and "How It Feels to Be Colored Me," her childhood habit of performing for whites who traveled on the road just outside the Eatonville gate. The young female protagonist of her autobiographical short story, "Drenched in Light," displays a similar proclivity. Clearly, these early events revealed her penchant for drama, but, again, her rugged individualism and keen intellect often did not serve her well in the collaborative work required for producing and staging plays. In 1930 she tried to collaborate on *Mule Bone* (a play) with Langston Hughes;[14] the attempted collaboration would end up driving a wedge between the two friends. In 1931 she wrote skits for a doomed theatrical review called *Fast and Furious*. In January of 1932 she wrote and staged another theatrical review, *The Great Day*, which premiered on Broadway at the John Golden Theatre on January 10. She also worked to produce a concert program under the auspices of the Creative Literature Department at Rollins College in Winter Park, Florida, and she staged *From Sun to Sun* (a version of *Great Day*) there in 1933. In 1934 she traveled to Bethune-Cookman College in Florida to establish a school of dramatic arts; she also saw the production of *Singing Steel* (another version of *Great Day*) in Chicago. In 1935 she joined the Works Progress Administration's Federal Theatre Project as a drama coach; she traveled to North Carolina in 1939 to work as a drama instructor at North Carolina College for Negroes (now North Carolina Central) at Durham. During this time, Hurston met famed University of North Carolina professor of drama, Paul Green.

Original scripts for ten Hurston plays deposited in the United States Copyright Office between 1925 and 1944 – all but one previously unproduced and unpublished before they appeared in *The Copyright Drama Deposit Collection* (1977) – are housed at the Library of Congress's Manuscript, Music, and Rare Books and Special Collections Division. Titles include "Cold Keener: A Review," "De Turkey and de Law: A Comedy in Three Acts," "Forty Yards," "Lawing and Jawing," "Meet the Mamma: A Musical Play in Three Acts," "The Mule-Bone: A Comedy of Negro Life in Three Acts," "Poker!," "Polk County: A Comedy of Negro Life on a Sawmill Camp with Authentic Negro Music in Three Acts," "Spunk" (also the title of the short story she published in *The New Negro*), and "Woofing."[15] Thus, we have abundant evidence of Hurston's strong, but perhaps unfulfilled, penchant for drama.

Hurston's busy teaching, research, production, and publishing schedule continued through the decade of the Great Depression. She even had time for a love affair with the man she called the love of her life, Percival Punter. Guggenheim Fellowships sponsored her travels to Jamaica and Haiti during 1936 and 1937 to collect folk materials that would result in *Tell My Horse* (1938). During her first trip to Haiti in 1936, Hurston wrote her best-known work, *Their Eyes Were Watching God* (1937) over a seven-week period. By April of 1938, she had joined a Federal Writers' Project in Florida to work on *The Florida Negro*. In 1939, she published "Now Take Noses" in *Cordially Yours*, received an honorary Doctor of Letters degree from Morgan State College, and published her third novel, *Moses, Man of the Mountain*.[16] Hurston's formal studies suffered as a result of all her other activities, and she failed to fulfill the requirements for the PhD in anthropology at Columbia. She simply did not have time to attend classes. She did, however, earn distinction as the most published black woman writer to emerge from that era, and she took the time for a second marriage – this time to the much younger Albert Price, III, on June 27, 1939, in Fernandina, Florida. They were divorced four years later on November 9, 1943.

Hurston traveled to South Carolina in the summer of 1940 to collect folklore; the following year she worked on her manuscript for *Dust Tracks on a Road*, published a short story in *Southern Literary Messenger*, and began a stint (October 1941 – January 1942) as a story consultant for Paramount Pictures. Her 1942 publications include *Dust Tracks on a Road*, "Story in Harlem Slang" in the *American Mercury*, and a profile of Lawrence Silas in the *Saturday Evening Post*. The following year *American Mercury* included "The 'Pet Negro' System" in its May issue, and *Negro Digest* published "My Most Humiliating Jim Crow Experience" in its June 1944 issue. According to Valerie Boyd, Hurston married again on January 18, 1944, this time to Cleveland businessman James Howell Pitts. The couple divorced eight months later on October 31, 1944. Meanwhile, Hurston continued to write. She wrote another novel, *Mrs. Doctor*, which dealt with upper-class blacks; however, her publisher, Bertram Lippincott, rejected it. She continued to have success with smaller pieces, including, "The Rise of the Begging Joints" in the March 1945 issue of *American Mercury*, "Crazy for This Democracy" in the December 1945 issue of *Negro Digest*, and a 1947 review of Robert Tallant's *Voodoo in New Orleans* in the *Journal of American Folklore*. October 1948 brought publication of her fourth novel, *Seraph on the Suwanee*.[17]

September 1948 began a devastating period for Hurston when she was arrested after being falsely accused of molesting a 10-year-old boy; the case was dismissed six months later, but the damage had been done. Though Hurston had endured race, gender, and other forms of prejudice for much of her life, the charge of molestation and the arrest surrounding it marked an ensuing period of decline in her professional life. Notwithstanding biographer Robert Hemenway's assessment that she returned to her usual exuberant and enthusiastic self after a brief period, Hurston's professional life clearly suffered after 1949. In the early 1950s, Hurston was working as a maid in Rivo Island, Florida; she published small articles in the *Saturday Evening Post* and *American Legion* magazine. In 1952, the *Pittsburgh Courier* hired Hurston to cover the Ruby McCollum matter, a highly publicized 1952 case in which a black woman was charged with the murder of her white lover. As the decade wore on, Hurston's politics became increasingly conservative, her rugged individualism never more evident than in her August 11, 1955 piece in the *Orlando Sentinel* criticizing the Supreme Court's decision in *Brown v. Board of Education of Topeka Kansas* (1954).[18]

She devoted substantial effort to a work on the life of Herod the Great but was unable to find a publisher for the manuscript. Between 1951 and 1956, she lived in Eau Gallie, Florida, on very modest earnings. Hemenway points out optimistically that despite her poverty, Hurston was essentially at peace during this time – though he acknowledges that the morals indictment had driven her to near suicide. According to Hemenway, Hurston subsisted in her final years on a meager income from substitute teaching and other jobs, which income was supplemented by welfare and unemployment benefits. In 1956, she began a job as a librarian at the Patrick Air Force Base in Florida, but she was fired in 1957. Between 1957 and 1959, she wrote "Hoodoo and Black Magic," a column for the *Fort Pierce Chronicle*. She also worked as a substitute teacher at Lincoln Park Academy in Fort Pierce, Florida, in 1958. Proud, alone, and without funds, the author simply worked until she could no longer produce. A stroke in 1959 forced her into the St. Lucie County (Florida) welfare home where she died the following year on January 28 of hypertensive heart disease. The woman who had appeared on the cover of the *Saturday Review* and who had during her lifetime been the recipient of numerous honors and awards, including a Rosenwald Foundation Fellowship, two Guggenheims, an Honorary Doctor of Letters Degree from Morgan State College, an Anisfeld-Wolf Book Award in Race Relations, the Howard University Distinguished Alumni Award, Bethune-Cookman College's Award for Education and Human Relations, was buried in an unmarked grave at Fort Pierce's segregated cemetery, the Garden of Heavenly Rest.

Alice Walker led the way toward Hurston's resurrection as a literary foremother just in time for the flowering of black women's literature during the final decades of the twentieth century. Hurston's work in the woman-centered narrative, particularly *Their Eyes Were Watching God*, connects African American women's literary production in the second half of the twentieth century and beyond to African American women's literary production in the nineteenth century. For example, the topic of black female sexuality so deftly explored in *Their Eyes Were Watching God* not only evokes Harriet Jacobs' *Incidents in the Life of a Slave Girl* (1861) and a history of black female sexual objectification, but it also looks ahead to Gwendolyn Brooks's *Maud Martha* (1956), Toni Morrison's *The Bluest Eye* (1970) and *Sula* (1974), Alice Walker's *The Color Purple* (1982), and even Alice Randall's *The Wind Done Gone* (2001). In her dedication of *I Love Myself When I Am Laughing and Then Again When I Am Looking Mean and Impressive* (1979), Walker describes Hurston in terms that she would later use to articulate her womanist aesthetic. At the same time, Hurston's literary resurrection became a central element in the second and third waves of black feminist thought, even as the literary world geared up to make her one of the most notable figures in American literary history and one of the five or six most recognized African American writers in the world. No survey or introductory level course on black women writers of the twentieth century would be complete without attention to her work.[19]

## Notes

1. The creek is the Sougahatchee River, often referred to as the Songahatchee River.
2. Boyd, *Wrapped in Rainbows*, p. 57.
3. *DTOAR* (1942; New York: HarperCollins, 1996), p. 87.
4. *Ibid.* p. 98.
5. Boyd, *Wrapped in Rainbows*, pp. 68–9.
6. Alain Locke, ed., *The New Negro: Voices of the Harlem Renaissance* (1925; New York: Atheneum, 1992).
7. Zora Neale Hurston, "John Redding Goes to Sea," 1921, *Zora Neale Hurston: The Complete Stories*, eds. Henry Louis Gates, Jr., and Sieglinde Lemke (New York: HarperCollins, 1995), pp. 1–16.
8. Zora Neale Hurston, "Drenched in Light," 1924, in Gates and Lemke, Zora Neale Hurston pp. 17–25.
9. Zora Neale Hurston, *MAM*, 1935, in *Zora Neale Hurston: Folklore, Memoirs, and Other Writings*, Cheryl Wall, ed. (New York: The Library of America, 1995), pp. 1–267; Hurston, *TMH*, 1938, in Wall, Zora Neale Hurston, pp. 269–555.
10. "Drenched in Light," 1924, in Gates and Lemke, *Zora Neale Hurston*, pp. 17–25; "Magnolia Flower," 1925, in Gates and Lemke, *Zora Neale Hurston*, pp. 33–40; "Spunk," 1925, in Gates and Lemke, *Zora Neale Hurston*, pp. 26–32; "Color Struck," *FIRE!!* 1 (November 1926), 7–15; "Sweat," 1926, in Gates and Lemke, *Zora Neale Hurston*, pp. 73–85.
11. *DTOAR*, p. 143.

12. "Cudjo's Own Story of the Last African Slaver," *Journal of Negro History* 12 (October 1927), 648–63.

13. "How It Feels to be Colored Me" in Cheryl A. Wall, ed., *Their Eyes Were Watching God: A Casebook*, (New York: Oxford University Press, 2000) pp. 826–9; Wallace Thurman, *Infants of the Spring* (1928) (Boston, MA: Northeastern Library of Black Literature, 1992); Hurston, "Hoodoo in America," *Journal of American Folklore* 44 (October–December 1931), 317–418; Hurston, "The Gilded Six-Bits," 1933, in Gates and Lemke, *Zora Neale Hurston*, pp. 86–98; Nancy Cunard, ed., *Negro: An Anthology* (1934; New York: Continuum, 1996); Hurston, *JGV* (New York: J. B. Lippincott, 1934); "The Fire and the Cloud," 1934, in Gates and Lemke, *Zora Neale Hurston*, pp. 117–21.

14. *Mule Bone: A Comedy of Negro Life*, eds. George Houston Bass and Henry Louis Gates, Jr. (New York: HarperPerennial, 1991).

15. Because no one renewed the copyright on these documents, they are in the public domain and available online at http://memory.loc.gov/ammem/znhhtml/znhhome.html.

16. TEWWG (1937; Urbana, IL, and Champaign, IL: University of Illinois Press, 1978); MMOTM (1939; Urbana, IL and Chicago, IL: University of Illinois Press, 1984).

17. "The 'Pet Negro' System" (1944), in Wall, *Their Eyes Were Watching God*, pp. 914–21; "My Most Humiliating Jim Crow Experience" (1944), in Wall, *Their Eyes Were Watching God*, pp. 935–6; "The Rise of the Begging Joints" (1945), in Wall, *Their Eyes Were Watching God*, pp. 937–49; "Crazy for This Democracy" (1945), in Wall, *Their Eyes Were Watching God*, pp. 945–9; SOTS (New York: Charles Scribner's Sons, 1948).

18. Zora Neale Hurston, "Court Order Can't Make Races Mix," (1955), *Zora Neale Hurston: Folklore Memoirs, and other Writings*, ed. Cheryl Wall (New York: Library of America, 1995), pp. 956–8.

19. Harriet Jacobs, *Incidents in the Life of a Slave Girl, Written by Herself* (1861), ed. Jean Fagan Yellin (Cambridge, MA: Harvard University Press, 1987); Toni Morrison, *Sula* (New York; Knopf, 1984); Alice Walker, *The Color Purple* (New York: Harcourt Brace Jovanovich, 1982); Alice Randall, *The Wind Done Gone* (Boston, MA: Houghton-Mifflin, 2001); Alice Walker, ed., *I Love Myself When I Am Laughing and Then Again When I Am Looking Mean and Impressive: A Zora Neale Hurston Reader* (New York: The Feminist Press, 1979), pp. 1–5.

# Chapter 2

# Contexts

This chapter examines historical, social, political, and cultural contexts for Zora Neale Hurston's life and work, from 1891 to 1960; some attention to the thirty-year period immediately preceding Hurston's birth is also important, for it encompasses one of the most turbulent and transformative periods in United States history: the Civil War (1861–1865) and its aftermath. Only twenty-six years separates the abolishment of chattel slavery in 1865 and the year of Hurston's birth. During that time-frame, the climate for most African Americans changed from great optimism during Radical Reconstruction, to feelings of betrayal and disillusionment by century's end.

During the Civil War, enslaved persons escaped by taking refuge with Union troops; they were subsequently labeled "contraband." Contraband relief organizations, such as Elizabeth Keckley's Contraband Relief Association based in Washington, DC, provided temporary assistance to these and other newly freedpersons who were, as one might expect, typically homeless and without basic means of support.[1] On March 3, 1865, Congress established the Freedmen's Bureau (Bureau of Freedmen, Refugees, and Abandoned Lands) in an effort to deal more comprehensively with the post-War and post-slavery chaos. The agency, which operated under the auspices of the War Department, functioned in a variety of ways to help freedpersons: it assisted in the establishment of schools and churches; it heard cases concerning labor disputes and criminal acts committed against African Americans; and it served as a clearinghouse for information that could assist in reuniting families. Initially, the Freedmen's Bureau operated on capital acquired from the sale and lease of property confiscated from former slaveholders, but that source of revenue was soon undermined by the Johnson administration's conservative policies. Though Abraham Lincoln's Emancipation Proclamation of 1863 freed a number of persons in rebelling states during the Civil War, slavery was not officially abolished in the United States until December of 1865 when the Thirteenth Amendment was finally ratified; it had been tied up in the legislature for well over a year. A fraction of the several million newly freed Americans briefly realized Union General Sherman's famous promise of land (often referred to as

"40 acres and a mule") for the heads of freed families in several states; however, most were forced to forfeit the land after President Andrew Johnson voided Sherman's promise in 1866.

In response to the Emancipation Proclamation and the Thirteenth Amendment, former Confederate states enacted Black Codes that served the ends of white supremacy in much the same manner as Slave Codes had served prior to the Civil War. Slave Codes had been used to define slavery and who could be enslaved, to justify the brutal treatment of enslaved persons, to deny them a voice in court proceedings, and generally to further constrict the lives of persons already enslaved. Though a few Black Codes were already in place before the Civil War, they proliferated in 1865 and 1866 to replace the social and other controls that the Emancipation Proclamation and the Thirteenth Amendment had removed. One major objective of Black Codes was to guarantee white planters an abundant supply of cheap (or free) labor. Blacks could be arrested for vagrancy and a variety of other minor charges and forced to labor on agricultural farms; or, they could be denied access to certain skilled trades and certain kinds of property. Children could be taken from their families and apprenticed to their former owners.

The climate for black Americans in the aftermath of the Civil War was decidedly hostile; after particularly bloody anti-black riots in Memphis, Tennessee, and New Orleans, Louisiana, the legislature authorized Radical Reconstruction. Under the Reconstruction Act of 1865, southern state governments were dissolved and federal military rule was installed. The Fourteenth and Fifteenth Amendments were ratified in 1868 and 1870, respectively, and effectively outlawed Black Codes. The Fourteenth Amendment granted rights of citizenship and due process to all persons born or naturalized in the United States, and the Fifteenth Amendment extended the franchise without regard to color or previous condition of servitude. With blacks outnumbering whites in some southern states, the Fifteenth Amendment paved the way for black men to be elected to political offices – and many were. Overall, such federal interventions disrupted to some degree the smooth operations of white supremacy and thus further angered an already humiliated south.

White supremacist groups such as the Ku Klux Klan, The White Brotherhood, Jayhawkers, The Pale Faces, and The Knights of the White Camellia emerged in this climate, launching campaigns of terror and intimidation. They often used lynching – a ritualistic mode of killing typically carried out by a mob – as a terror tactic. The lynching ritual involved much more than hanging; it could include tarring and feathering, mutilation, beating, or other forms of torture. Lynchings of African Americans increased steadily in the decades following the Civil War, peaking in the early 1890s (when Hurston was a mere toddler), and continuing steadily well into the first half of the twentieth century. African Americans responded with an anti-lynching crusade, and two of its most prominent workers were Ida B. Wells-Barnett (1862–1931) and Walter White (1893–1955).

Wells-Barnett was an educator before her partnership in *The Free Speech and Headlight*, a Memphis, Tennessee, newspaper, became lucrative enough for her to focus solely on journalism. As activist and organizer, Wells-Barnett was associated with a number of black women's clubs and organizations, and she joined the fight for universal suffrage. She was also involved with W. E. B. Du Bois and others in forming the Niagara Movement, which became the National Association for the Advancement of Colored People (NAACP). Her interest in documenting the circumstances surrounding lynchings intensified after a mob of whites murdered her friends Thomas Moss, Calvin McDowell, and Will Stewart in 1892. She traveled extensively, investigating lynchings and publishing her findings in titles such as *Southern Horrors: Lynch Law in All Its Phases* (1892), *A Red Record: Tabulated Statistics and Alleged Causes of Lynchings in the United States, 1892–1893–1894* (1895), and *Mob Rule in New Orleans: Robert Charles and His Fight to the Death* (1900).[2] Walter White, who was light enough to pass for white and could thus investigate lynchings from an insider's perspective, was drawn into the crusade against lynching after witnessing atrocities committed during the Atlanta, Georgia, race riot of 1906. White joined the NAACP in 1918, directing much of his energy toward the anti-lynching crusade; he became executive director of the NAACP in 1929.

The specter of lynching found its way into novels, poems, plays, essays, and speeches in the late nineteenth and early twentieth centuries. Frances Ellen Watkins Harper's *Iola Leroy* (1892), which borrowed its title character's first name from Ida B. Wells-Barnett's pen name, incorporated the topic through dialogue and plot. Likewise, James Weldon Johnson made the witnessing of a lynching the chief reason for his unnamed protagonist's decision to pass for white in *The Autobiography of an Ex-Coloured Man* (1912). Concern about lynching spawned a subgenre of African American drama – the anti-lynching play, with some of the best plays coming from authors such as Angelina Weld Grimke and Georgia Douglas Johnson. Literary critic Trudier Harris offers a comprehensive treatment of America's lynching phenomenon in *Exorcising Blackness: Historical and Literary Lynching and Burning Rituals* (1984). In addition, numerous nonfiction works examine the lynching phenomenon in America between the Civil War and the mid-twentieth century, when one of the nation's most notorious lynchings occurred – that of 14-year-old Emmett Louis Till in Money, Mississippi, in 1955.[3]

Despite the hostile socio-political climate of the late nineteenth century, Congress consistently refused to pass a federal law outlawing lynching. Recognizing that a campaign of intimidation and other practices (including the poll tax and the grandfather clause) had effectively removed the power of the franchise from black voters and thus undermined any chance for his re-election, George White – the last black member remaining in Congress in 1900 – submitted an anti-lynching bill to the Judiciary Committee; the measure was soundly defeated. After White's departure, another 28 years would pass before an African American would again be elected to serve in Congress. In October of 2005 Congress officially apologized for its failure to enact a federal anti-lynching law during the almost 100-year reign of domestic terrorism. While enslaved blacks had been characterized as peculiarly childlike and appropriate for slavery in antebellum America, they were often depicted as morally retrograde and, therefore, dangerous in the late nineteenth century. Lynching was one approach to eradicating the so-called black menace.

African American writers, speakers, critics, and activists saw it as their most immediate task and imperative duty to challenge and counter such stigmatizing discourse. Even before the Civil War had ended, William Wells Brown (1814–1884) – who had escaped from slavery and subsequently wrote and published in several genres – used his writing to provide evidence that would vindicate black America's much maligned character. Author and activist Frances Ellen Watkins Harper (1825–1911) called for a spirit of cooperation and collective effort among African Americans to ward off racially oppressive social and political phenomena. The racial uplift theme in her speeches and nonfiction found its way into her fiction and poetry. Her involvement with uplift projects began during the antebellum period and continued through the end of the nineteenth century. Typically the province of African Americans espousing middle-class values, racial uplift programs were designed to assist in raising the living conditions of black Americans through various strategies of moral and practical education. Harper made the uplift formula central to *Trial and Triumph* (1888–1889), a novel that features an archetypal orphaned protagonist of tender age who is transformed from an errant child to a proper young woman and community servant because of the nurturance she receives from the church, the school, the community, and her hardworking, self-sacrificing, and morally upstanding grandmother.

A number of other prominent African Americans, such as cultural critic Victoria Earle Matthews (1861–1907) and magazine editor Pauline Hopkins (1859–1930), felt that African Americans must use their writing to counteract the effects of racism and racist representations in American culture. Much of the fiction produced by African Americans during this unique period in American history took care to present African Americans in their best light and/or to offer a blueprint for approaching life from a strong ethical base; exemplary protagonists, whose quest for self-actualization included the desire to be recognized as fully human and intelligent beings, demonstrated that they possessed the requisite character and ability to be productive American citizens. That factor notwithstanding, works such as Harper's *Iola Leroy*, Hopkins' *Contending Forces* (1900), Paul Laurence Dunbar's *The Sport of the Gods* (1902), and Charles Chesnutt's *The House Behind the Cedars* (1900), *The Marrow of Tradition* (1901), and others often included an accompanying critique of the white-supremacist mindset, moral hypocrisy, and the absurdity of using the color line to determine and measure human value.[4]

In national politics, the period from 1874 to 1888 turned increasingly toward states' rights because of Supreme Court decisions handed down under the leadership of Chief Justice Morrison Remick Waite. Waite struck down parts of the 1875 Civil Rights Act and turned over to states the regulation of public accommodations, a scenario that helped set the stage for the Supreme Court decision in *Plessy v. Ferguson* (1896). During the same period, an important education bill introduced by Republican Senator Henry W. Blair in 1876 was held up for over a decade and finally defeated in 1890. The bill would have allowed for federal funding of public education without regard to race. Congress also defeated the Force Bill, which would have worked toward honest federal elections. The defeat of the Force Bill made it easier for states and localities to deny the vote to African American men (since women were not granted the franchise until 1920) through poll taxes, grandfather clauses, and other measures.

Charles Chesnutt (1858–1932) – almost two generations older than Hurston – made voting rights central to *The Marrow of Tradition*. He based the story on events relating to the massacre of African Americans in Wilmington, North Carolina, following the 1898 election. After African Americans exercised their right to vote, untold numbers of them were murdered and/or driven from their homes and property; the result of the riot was a severely changed demographic in Wilmington which, prior to the violence, boasted a large black, propertied population that held substantial potential for challenging white political dominance. Chesnutt set his fictionalized version of the riot *before* the election rather than *after* it. His work stands alongside that of other authors, such as Harper's *Trial and Triumph* and *Iola Leroy*, and Sutton Griggs's *Imperium in Imperio* (1899), in taking particular note of the political barriers to African American progress in the decades following Emancipation. Hurston (born some fourteen years after the official dismantling of

Reconstruction) came of age during this period of social and political reversal for African Americans.

Historian Rayford W. Logan and others have characterized the period between 1890 and 1915 as the nadir, or lowest point, for African Americans. Jim Crow segregation had been federalized by the *Plessy* decision in 1896. While historians associate early uses of the term "Jim Crow" with a song title, "Jump Jim Crow," and a 1930s black-face minstrel performance by Thomas Rice, in later years the term came to signify laws and customs that facilitated racial segregation. Black codes had been dissolved through federal enactments under Radical Reconstruction; however, southern states had taken advantage of pro-states' rights-era decisions and passed segregation statutes that would be tested and ultimately upheld through *Plessy*. The *Plessy* case derived its name from the light-skinned Creole activist – Homère Patrick Plessy (1863–1925) – who served a role similar to that served by Rosa Parks in the 1955 act of civil disobedience that incited the Montgomery, Alabama, Bus Boycott. Passengers on Louisiana railroads had been free to ride in any car since 1867, but in 1890 Louisiana passed the Separate Car Act, segregating its railroad facilities. Plessey was one of a number of persons who volunteered to test the law. On June 7, 1892, he boarded a White Only car of the East Louisiana Railroad line and was subsequently dragged off and arrested. He was found guilty, but appeals led all the way to the famous Supreme Court decision that bears his name. With one lone dissenter in Justice Harlan, the *Plessy* court held that separation of the races violated neither the Thirteenth nor the Fourteenth Amendment so long as equal facilities were provided without regard to race. The ruling was easily co-opted in the service of white supremacy.

In addition to setbacks in the legislative and judicial realms, the social situation at the end of the nineteenth century included the continued virtual re-enslavement of numerous persons through the penal/prison-farm system (which Black Codes had facilitated immediately following the Civil War). Typically segregated by race well into the twentieth century, inmates in such systems performed a variety of agricultural and other tasks that generated resources for the state and/or for private enterprises. In a number of states, prisoners (men and women, the overwhelming majority of which were African American) were subjected to the convict-lease system, a process by which they were leased to a specific landowner. The system boasted a high mortality rate. In the early 1900s, Tennessee plantation owner Joe Turner became notorious for illegally enslaving black men through the penal-labor system for his own financial gain. A famous Blues title, "Joe Turner's Come and Gone" (also the title of an August Wilson play) captures the sentiment of Blues-ridden black families deprived of the men in their lives through unjust incarcerations. The theme would reverberate in African American literature throughout the twentieth century in works such as James Baldwin's *Go Tell It on the Mountain* (1953), *If Beale Street Could Talk* (1974), *Tell Me How Long the Train's Been Gone* (1968), and Toni Morrison's *Beloved* (1987), among others.[5]

Varieties of tenant farming represented another form of re-enslavement that continued to exploit labor several generations beyond the official end of slavery. In the late nineteenth century, planters had plenty of land but they no longer had a free supply of labor to work it. Formerly enslaved persons, possessing neither property nor source of livelihood, needed a means of subsistence. Tenant farming developed from this socio-economic situation. In one system, tenants could rent or lease a parcel of land and either retain the profits from the resources produced or share the profits with the landowner. Another arrangement involved sharecropping, where the landowner furnished tenants with food, clothing, materials, and housing. Tenant and landowner then shared the profits of the harvest, with the tenant being responsible for reimbursing the landowner for the cost of food, clothing, materials, and housing. Arrangements varied in their terms and sometimes land-leasing arrangements included an initial outlay of operating capital.

Hurston situates the opening segments of *Jonah's Gourd Vine* in a tenant-farming household around 1880; the plot displays (to some degree) several varieties of tenant-farming experiences through a comparison of the particularly brutal situation of the Crittenden household with that of the families that work for Alfred Pearson on the other side of the Songahatchee River. Character Ned Crittenden mentions binding protagonist John Buddy over to a cruel planter named Mimms and, at one point in the story, the Crittenden household moves from its initial tenant-farming situation to the Shelby plantation, which they feel will be better. The novel provides a record of how versions of the plantation system continued with the exploitation of black labor in the generations following the official end of slavery, though, in Booker T. Washington (1856–1915) form, Hurston avoids indicting the system and instead offers (through John Pearson) an example of the radical transcendent individual. Protagonist John Pearson escapes the tenant-farming system through his hard work, talent, and support from his (white) father and (most importantly) his wife Lucy Potts. He prospers and effectively spends his entire life casting down his bucket in the soil of the south.

The character (who is based on Hurston's father) exemplifies the vision for the masses of black southerners that Washington articulated in his famous 1895 "Atlanta Exposition Speech," a speech later incorporated into *Up from Slavery* (1901).[6] In the speech, Washington urged southern African Americans to cast down their buckets in the soil of the south rather than seek prosperity elsewhere. He reminded white southerners and would-be philanthropists of their options: some 16 million hands serving as an asset or some 16 million hands serving as a liability. Washington's publicly articulated vision offered no direct or explicit counter to the segregationist discourse of the Supreme Court in *Plessy* or to prevailing white-supremacist ideology in general. In addition to telling the story of Washington's ascent from slavery, *Up from Slavery* set out his agenda for African American economic progress through vocational education and training.

In the year of Hurston's birth, Washington was emerging as the preeminent black spokesperson in the United States. Prior to his ascent, Frederick Douglass (1818–1895), who escaped from Maryland slavery in 1838, had been the best-known spokesperson for blacks before, during, and after the Civil War. Washington had also been born into slavery, in Virginia; freed after the Civil War, he eventually worked his way through Hampton Normal (Teaching) and Agricultural Institute (now Hampton University) in Virginia. In addition to serving as Washington's alma mater, Hampton was founded as an HBCU (historically black college or university[7]) in 1868 by Brigadier General Samuel Armstrong with the help of the American Missionary Association (AMA). The AMA assisted in founding several black colleges and teaching schools between 1861 and 1870. Though HBCUs were founded in large part because most of America's institutions of higher learning did not admit African Americans, and though many now suffer financially, such schools would eventually become the primary producers of black leaders and professionals. Like Hampton, many of these schools also received funding from the Freedmen's Bureau.

Hampton founder Armstrong shared a common philosophy with Washington about how to move black Americans away from slavery and toward becoming productive members of society. Both men felt that practical training in a vocation resulting in gainful employment was the best approach to resolving the problem at hand and, importantly, neither man wanted to push for social equality for black Americans. Those who favored more radical approaches to America's race problem saw Washington's plan as accommodationist because of its compromise on social equality, which would have entailed the full enjoyment of the rights and privileges associated with citizenship. Washington's conservative approach to socio-economic progress for African Americans so appealed to Armstrong that, by 1881, he had recommended Washington to head Tuskegee Institute in Alabama. Washington details his Tuskegee experience in *Up from Slavery*, explaining how his personal qualities of frugality, industry, and honesty earned him the respect and trust of potential donors whose gifts would change Tuskegee from a school with no buildings (only a dilapidated shed in 1881) to a significant institution of black higher education with 100 faculty members and numerous buildings by 1900. Washington knew how to appeal to rich philanthropists who might donate money for African American education – often with the understanding that funding was contingent on the degree to which schools specialized in industrial or vocational education over liberal arts education. His prominence was due in no small part to his ability to negotiate within the parameters set by the moneyed and powerful.

Washington's primary rival for the role of black spokesperson was W. E. B. Du Bois (1868–1963). Both men were dedicated to progress for African Americans; however, Du Bois and many others did not feel that education for African Americans should be limited to vocational training. Nor did they agree with Washington's position on social equality, his seeming acquiescence to Jim Crow segregation and the denial of full citizenship rights and privileges to African Americans. Washington would, nevertheless, enjoy the central leadership role until his death in 1915, just as African Americans geared up for what has come to be known as the Great Migration away from the south. Hurston would turn 24 that year and begin her travels with a Gilbert and Sullivan acting troupe; her travels would end at Baltimore, Maryland, where she found a way to continue her formal education at two other HBCUs – Morgan Academy (now Morgan State University) and Howard University.

While Washington had urged African Americans to stay in the south despite the hostile social and political climate, the campaign to malign the character of African Americans and to maintain white supremacy and Jim Crow rule continued. White Baptist preacher Tom Dixon produced three of the most influential works of the early twentieth century: *The Leopard's Spots: A Romance of the White Man's Burden* (1902), *The Clansman: An Historical Romance of the Ku Klux Klan* (1905), and *The Traitor: A Story of the Fall of the Invisible Empire* (1907).[8] While the first novel in Dixon's trilogy was a direct response to what Dixon deemed inaccurate representations of race relations in Harriet Beecher Stowe's *Uncle Tom's Cabin* (1852),[9] the novel was so well received by American audiences that Dixon decided to write two more novels casting African Americans as the evil menace corrupting America's white paradise. His work – particularly *The Clansman* – served as the source material for D. W. Griffith's groundbreaking film, *The Birth of a Nation* (1915). A major hit among white audiences, the explicitly racist film endorsed slavery and the suppression of African Americans while supporting the Ku Klux Klan and white supremacy in general. African Americans were caricatured as beasts and rapists who threatened white supremacy, with Klan members depicted as saviors and protectors. The film was re-released several times before 1939 when *Gone with the Wind* (the film adaptation of Margaret Mitchell's 1936 novel) displaced it as the most popular film in the United States. The release and subsequent re-releases of *The*

*Birth of a Nation* incited riots, lawsuits, and all manner of organized protest – including vociferous protest from the NAACP. While Mitchell's *Gone with the Wind*'s major accomplishment was that it offered a revision of white southern womanhood, its depictions of African Americans and race relations in general rehashed nostalgic pre-Civil War white American images of African Americans as happy or contented slaves, and white masters and mistresses as their benevolent and patient superiors. Mitchell's novel and film (whose racism is much more subtle than that of the novel) had in common with Dixon's work and Griffith's film the problematic post-War depictions of African Americans as dangerous and retrograde with the concomitant endorsement of white mob action. Still, African Americans were less outraged by *Gone with the Wind* than they had been with *The Birth of a Nation* and were able to applaud Hattie McDaniel's winning of the Academy Award for her role as Mammy.[10]

Booker T. Washington died the same year that *The Birth of a Nation* appeared, and W. E. B. Du Bois continued his rise to prominence. Du Bois brought a black northern perspective to America's racial problems just in time for the Great Migration that resulted in large African American populations in northern urban centers. Some twelve years younger than Washington, Du Bois was born in Great Barrington, Massachusetts. Growing up as one of very few African Americans in Great Barrington, Du Bois was more accustomed to muted racial innuendo than the overt racism he encountered while he attended college from 1885 to 1888 at Fisk College (another HBCU, now Fisk University), in Nashville, Tennessee. The discrimination he witnessed during that initial period in the south drove his determination to devote his life to the cause of racial justice. After graduating from Fisk, Du Bois entered Harvard University with junior status and earned his baccalaureate degree in 1890 – the year before Hurston was born. In 1895 he became the first African American to receive a Harvard PhD. His dissertation, *The Suppression of the African Slave Trade in America* (1896) became the first volume in Harvard's renowned Historical Series. A prolific author, Du Bois published numerous other volumes; his best-known work remains *The Souls of Black Folks*, considered central to the canon of African American literature. It was in this volume that Du Bois made his famous pronouncement that the problem of the twentieth century would be that of the color line.[11]

Du Bois had been one of the founding members of the Niagara Movement, which began as a series of meetings near Niagara Falls in upstate New York and Canada and ultimately became the NAACP in 1909. The men and women who organized the Niagara Movement denounced Booker T. Washington's accommodationist logic, lobbied against Jim Crow policies, and demanded the full and complete suffrage rights that had been extended to black men by the Fifteenth Amendment to the Constitution in 1870. As editor of the NAACP journal, *Crisis*, Du Bois set its publishing agenda, which included news and commentary about social issues (including lynching) and African American cultural production. In 1926, the journal was offering a regular discussion forum on the criteria for Negro art, with established authors and emerging writers weighing in. By the time Hurston was beginning to make a name for herself among the Harlem literati, Du Bois had become a leading member of the black literary establishment. In "Criteria of Negro Art" (1926), Du Bois asserted, among other things, that all art is propaganda and his art would always be political. He was the quintessential race man; he believed strongly in organized collective action against race-based discrimination and oppression.

It was inevitable that Du Bois and Hurston would diverge on some key issues relating to art, politics, and race matters. Hurston was a lifelong Republican who grew increasingly conservative in her later years, while the masses of black Americans became increasingly Democratic.[12] Hurston was not a strong supporter of collective action such as that represented by uplift programs and pursued through a variety of organizations such as the NAACP and the Urban League (an organization that began around 1910 in response to a growing black presence in northern cities). Hurston, largely influenced by Enlightenment reasoning, believed in radical individualist effort as a way to overcome and transcend America's social ills. In her artistic production, she was staunchly individualistic even writing within the constraints of a white publishing industry. Du Bois was never a fan of Hurston's work, and when she wrote a lengthy and detailed letter to Du Bois (to whom she often referred secretly as "Dr. Dubious") in 1945 to ask that he spearhead a campaign to raise money for a black artists' cemetery in Florida, the two had not spoken for two decades. He responded in one sentence that he was too busy to take up the matter. His uplift agenda, his criteria for *proper* African American art, his vision of a leadership vanguard (a Talented Tenth), and his preference for organized, collective action would have made for a problematic close relationship with Hurston. Certainly, even as she tried to negotiate the racism and sexism she encountered in the publishing world, Hurston resisted the kind of prescriptive control over her artistic production that Du Bois and others advocated.

For example, in writing her best-known woman character, Janie Crawford, Hurston resisted the influence of dominant nineteenth-century ideologies of womanhood that were still impacting literary production in the twentieth century. In the nineteenth century, true womanhood ideology placed black women on the licentious end of a spectrum against its opposite: bourgeois white women, who exhibited the qualities of domesticity, piety, *purity*, and submissiveness – true women. The bourgeois wife was placed on a pedestal, which had the simultaneous effect of protecting and constricting. Working-class women, in large part because they were forced to operate outside the protected domestic sphere of hearth and home, were stigmatized as being less virtuous than so-called true women. In her nineteenth-century essays and speeches, Frances Ellen Watkins Harper called for true men *as well as* true women. The New Woman Movement, comprised primarily of white middle-class women who wanted changes in etiquette, dress, and options for self-actualization that were not limited to marriage and motherhood, offered another mode of response. Some New Women went so far as to challenge the idea that women were inherently maternal and nurturing. Though women had lobbied for suffrage long before the rise of the New Woman, the movement is often considered a predecessor to the suffrage movement that ended in passage of the Nineteenth Amendment to the Constitution in 1920.

Another response to true womanhood ideology was more mixed; the Black Women's Club Movement, developed independent of, but concurrently with, the New Women Movement in the late nineteenth century. Club leaders took as a primary mission in their uplift project the task of creating employment opportunities for black women that would allow them to avoid work situations where their sexual virtue could be easily compromised or undermined.[13] Part of the catalyst for their response was the fact that dominant patriarchal discourse often reduced black female sexuality to licentiousness, setting black women up as easy prey for abuse and exploitation in public spaces – including the workplace. Such a notion of black womanhood derived from centuries of European encounters with Africans and found peculiarly rich soil in the climate of sexual and reproductive abuse and exploitation that was part of American chattel slavery. Thus, part of the downside of rescuing their collective moral virtue was that clubwomen often adopted or *bought into* dominant ideologies of womanhood that precluded certain classes of black women from participation in their activities. One result of the Club Movement's response to demeaning and stigmatizing discourse about black female sexuality was that black female sexuality itself became muted or obliterated altogether in *proper* public discourse, including African American literature and art.

Hurston dealt with the issue of black female sexuality (and discourses that served to circumscribe it) in much of her work, most notably *Their Eyes Were Watching God*. Janie's recollection of Nanny's story of sexual exploitation under slavery and Janie's mother's rape in freedom collectively signify the narrow conception (historically) of African American female sexuality. Nanny's experiences and those of her daughter guide her acceptance (to some degree) of dominant ideologies of womanhood and her attempt to suppress Janie's sexual expression. Hurston constructs heroine Janie Mae Crawford Killicks Starks Woods as a sexually desiring subject who insists on making sexual expression part of her quest for experience and self-knowledge.

Though Janie's physical depiction (as light-skinned with long "good" hair) did not stray from the black literary establishment's aesthetic criteria for black heroines, Hurston refused to make her mulatto character tragic as they had often been depicted. In the late nineteenth and early twentieth centuries, the mixed-race or mulatto character appeared in stories about individuals who often faced the question of whether they should pass for white and open up a world of opportunity and social mobility, or identify as black in order to, among other things, serve the cause of racial uplift. Earlier, the heroine (or, occasionally, hero) was featured tragically as someone who faced a crisis of identity or a reversal of fortune upon being exposed as black. The mixed-race character also called attention to America's history of sexual relations across the color line, a line made more rigid and pronounced by Jim Crow segregation. Laws relating to race-mixing date back to the colonial era, though the term "miscegenation" (which derives from the Latin words *miscere* and *genus*), came into use around the time of the Emancipation Proclamation. In the nineteenth century, some thirty-eight states enacted (anti)miscegenation statutes for the primary purpose of outlawing interracial marriage, though some northern states repealed their statutes during the Civil War and several southern states (including Mississippi, Louisiana, and South Carolina) temporarily removed their bans on interracial marriage. In the final decade of Hurston's life, some twenty-nine miscegenation statutes remained active; the Supreme Court's 1967 decision in *Loving v. Virginia* ruled such statutes unconstitutional.[14] Despite bans on interracial liaisons, the evidence of cross-racial sexual relations is apparent in the many shades of African Americans that existed during and after slavery. Indeed, as Lawrence Otis Graham notes in *Our Kind of People: Inside America's Black Upper Class* (1999), the African American upper class owes much of its membership to America's history of cross-racial liaisons. It is no accident that so many upper-class African Americans are light-skinned, having benefited as descendents of propertied white men who (sometimes) provided well for their mixed-race offspring.

As the twentieth century moved forward, black Americans migrated to northern cities in droves. Between 1910 and 1930, the black population in the south *decreased* by over a million, while the black population in the north *increased* by over a million. Large numbers of black Americans left the south because they were fed up with decades of Jim Crow segregation and the terrorism of radical white supremacists. The racially oppressive socio-economic climate in the early twentieth century resulted in a number of race riots across the south and in the north, in cities such as New Orleans, Louisiana, in 1900, Atlanta, Georgia, in 1906, East St. Louis, Illinois, in 1917, and Chicago, Illinois, in 1919. African Americans faced stiff competition for jobs in the north because new European immigrants were arriving daily; they also faced mob violence when they were used as union-breakers. Black male unemployment in northern urban areas was oppressively high, and domestic work was the most prevalent type of non-agricultural employment available to black women. African Americans in the north and south persevered under the harsh socio-economic conditions, however. Some, like Hurston's family before her mother's death, managed to acquire and hold on to real estate; a black middle class emerged, with a few families managing to achieve wealth that could be passed down through subsequent generations. Nevertheless, the masses, many of whom were still less than two generations beyond slavery, continued to face formidable barriers to social mobility and economic prosperity in the early twentieth century.

The period is also marked by World War I (1914–1918), sometimes called the Great War, or the War to End All Wars. The two sides in the conflict were represented by the Central Powers (Austria-Hungary, Germany, and the Ottoman Empire [Turkey]) and the Allies (the United States, Belgium, France, Great Britain, Serbia, and Russia). Early engagements began in Eastern Europe in 1914; over the next few years, the conflict spread across Europe and to Great Britain. The United States entered the war in April 6, 1917 when it declared war on Germany for sinking US ships. African American soldiers, eager to demonstrate their willingness to fight for America, and hopeful that their service would lead to full citizenship, ultimately served mostly supporting roles in segregated units. Of some 367,000 black soldiers serving during World War I only about 10 percent actually saw conflict. The NAACP, only eight years old in 1917, protested the separate and unequal assignments and the abuse (including lynching) of black soldiers. Some 1,300 black soldiers who served in the war were eventually commissioned and promoted to officers. Following World War I, for a brief period before the economic downturn of the 1930s, Harlem (like other urban areas) flourished.

Harlem, in particular, was a place of hope and celebration for African Americans. It was, after all, the advent of the Jazz Age and the site of the cultural phenomenon that has come to be known as the Harlem Renaissance. Though many black artists were based in the Washington, DC area and elsewhere, Harlem was *the* place to be in the 1920s. Hurston arrived just as Alain Locke (1886–1954) was articulating his vision of a shifting paradigm from highly prescriptive uplift literature to literature that represented a renaissance in black American culture, a cultural and social transformation "of the inner and outer life of the Negro in America."[15] Locke expressed his vision in the fore-word to *The New Negro* (1925). The phrase, "the new Negro," had appeared decades earlier in an 1895 editorial in the *Cleveland Gazette* in reference to middle-class African Americans who demanded their full rights as United States citizens. Author Sutton Elbert Griggs (1872–1933) also used the phrase in *Imperium in Imperio* (1899): "The cringing, fawning, sniffling, cowardly Negro which slavery left, had disappeared, and a New Negro, self-respecting, fearless, and determined in the assertion of his rights was at hand."[16] The phrase also appeared as the title of a 1916 essay collection by William Pickens (1881–1954).

First published as an edition of the journal *Survey Graphic*, Locke's volume contains the work of some of the most talented and memorable artists of that period, including Jean Toomer, Langston Hughes, Hurston, Anne Spencer, James Weldon Johnson, Countee Cullen, and Jessie Fauset. Comprised of essays, drama, visual art, fiction, and poetry, the volume is divided into two parts: "The Negro Renaissance," and "The New Negro in a New World." Locke notes that the "Old Negro" is more myth than man, more formula than human being, a "stock figure perpetuated as an historical fiction partly in innocent sentimentalism, partly in deliberate reactionism."[17] In addition, just as Booker T. Washington had brokered much of the funding for black education during his time, Alain Locke served as the liaison for artists and the patronage they needed in order to have time to work; male artists were privileged under this arrangement. He declared the New Negro vibrant, awake, and progressive.

The period was not without its debates and controversies surrounding the criteria for the new literature, however. W. E. B. Du Bois believed black artists had a duty to be political and to represent black people positively, while many younger artists wanted an end to the prescriptive aesthetics of the past. Wallace Thurman (1902–1934) did not believe art should come with any agenda, and Claude McKay (1889–1948) denounced the prize-giving and official grooming of artists such as had been Hurston's experience; neither did he condone Du Bois's reasoning that all art was propaganda. Like Thurman, McKay felt that the artist who set out with a political agenda had already undermined his true artistic expression. For Locke, politics was present in the existence of the black artist and his work. Locke wanted African Americans to follow that approach while writing about their own experiences in those forms. Author and critic George Schuyler (1895–1977) asserted that there was no such thing as Negro art. He nevertheless authored guidelines for literary production that included specific criteria for representing black people and their lives. Langston Hughes' contribution to the conversation came in the form of an artist's manifesto in which he essentially took the position that Negro art did indeed exist, and it was up to the artist to decide what his or her art would be. He eschewed prescription, stating that he cared not whether anyone approved of his art so long as he was free to create it in his own way. Though a number of artists were gay or bisexual (or in the case of Langston Hughes, rumored to be so), very little space was given to public representation of anything other than heterosexuality in literature and art. Younger artists in quest of greater freedom attempted their own literary magazine, *FIRE!!* Edited by ascerbic novelist and critic Thurman, the first and only issue of the magazine featured drawings, poems, short stories, and essays by Aaron Douglass, Langston Hughes, Helene Johnson, Hurston, Thurman, and others. It also contained one of the first overtly gay-themed works published by a black American writer: Richard Bruce Nugent's "Smoke, Lilies and Jade, a Novel, Part I." Obviously, Du Bois did not approve of the journal.

According to Locke, the literature produced during the Harlem Renaissance would be "of" the Negro, rather than *about the Negro problem*: "We turn therefore in the other direction to the elements of truest social portraiture, and discover in the artistic self-expression of the Negro to-day a new figure on the national canvas and a new force in the foreground of affairs. . . . So far as he is culturally articulate, we shall let the Negro speak for himself."[18] His words seemed to speak directly to the kind of work Hurston wanted to produce; however, Hurston's experiences as a black woman negotiating space for her voice between the white-male-dominated publishing world and a male-dominated black literary establishment and patronage system were decidedly more difficult than Locke's statements would have us believe. As Cheryl Wall notes in *The Women of the Harlem Renaissance* (1995), Locke's paradigm simultaneously "overstates the case for male writers" while contradicting "the experience of many women."[19] The Stock Market crash only four years later meant less patronage for artists and writers, regardless of sex, and most of the women authors writing during the period were seriously overshadowed by their male counterparts. Jessie Fauset (1882–1961) was one of the more successful women writers who served as literary editor for *Crisis* and published four novels: *There Is Confusion* (1924), *Plum Bun* (1929), *The Chinaberry Tree* (1931), and *Comedy: American Style* (1933). Nella Larsen (1893–1964) had her primary contributions – *Quicksand* (1928) and *Passing* (1929) – come during the year that marks the beginning of the Great Depression.

With Locke's anthology serving as the movement's inaugural and seminal document, several decades would pass before African American women scholars and authors began the process of recovering their literary foremothers and illuminating their many contributions to the tradition of African American literature. Richard Wright (1908–1960), a Hurston contemporary and antagonist (who wrote a blistering review of Hurston and *Their Eyes Were Watching God*) came to prominence in the late 1930s. Wright wrote an important critical essay on the criteria for black American literary production, "Blueprint for Negro Writing" (1937) and followed up with *Uncle Tom's Children* (1938), *Native Son* (1940), and *Black Boy* (1945). Like a number of other artists – Claude McKay, Jessie Fauset, Langston Hughes, Chester Himes, and James Baldwin – Wright left America in search of greater personal and artistic freedom. After moving to France, he published several other volumes, including *The Outsider* (1953), *Savage Holiday* (1954), and *The Long Dream* (1958).

While the New Negro Movement served as the backdrop for a few of Hurston's early literary achievements, five of her seven books were published during the decade following the October 1929 Stock Market crash – the period known as the Great Depression. American industry had been in full force by the time World War I began; the war only served to enhance American industry, creating a gap between America's capacity for production and its capacity for consumption. People of means sunk their money into stocks and real estate and, when the market crashed, they suffered great financial losses. Businesses and factories closed, banks failed, and unemployment rose to 25 percent by 1932. Herbert Clark Hoover (1874–1964), a Republican, had been President for less than a year when the market crashed, but he would ultimately be blamed for the severe economic downturn.

Hoover, who believed that relief should happen at the local level, rather than the federal level, was defeated by Democrat Franklin D. Roosevelt (1882–1945) in a 1932 landslide. Roosevelt felt that action was required on the federal level in order to turn the country's economy around. He instituted what he called a New Deal for Americans immediately after his inauguration. Under his administration, banking reform laws were passed and emergency relief programs were established, as were the Social Security Act and the Federal Deposit Insurance Corporation. Other efforts included work relief programs – such as the Works Progress Administration (WPA) and the Civilian Conservation Corps (CCC) – and agricultural programs. While Roosevelt's New Deal programs made him immensely popular and he was elected for three terms, some of his more hastily instituted or poorly administered programs were ripe for strong criticism.

Zora Neale Hurston and other authors associated with the Harlem Renaissance worked on the Federal Writers' Project (FWP) under the auspices of the WPA. The FWP included a Folklore section for collecting songs, stories, and traditions, with a specific emphasis on preserving folk traditions for ensuing generations. The Florida FWP, for which Hurston worked, was based in Jacksonville and oversaw a number of recording expeditions; Hurston was involved in several of these. Interestingly, Hurston chose not to discuss the WPA in her autobiography, perhaps feeling some disdain about having had to rely on relief – though clearly it was her relief checks that made it possible for her to be so productive during this period; she managed to publish *Jonah's Gourd Vine, Mules and Men, Their Eyes Were Watching God, Tell My Horse,* and *Moses, Man of the Mountain* and followed up with her autobiography only two years into the 1940s.

During the Great Depression, it was not unusual for people to travel (illegally) by freight train from locale to locale in search of employment. In 1931, a group of black teenagers falsely accused of raping two young white women as they all rode on freight trains in search of work were arrested and thrown into jail in Scottsboro, Alabama. They became known as the Scottsboro Boys, and their lives were irreparably damaged by the charges and resultant series of litigations that continued through most of the 1930s. Some of the young men were eventually acquitted, but others served brutal prison time until they were eligible for parole. See, for example, Dan T. Carter's, *Scottsboro: A Tragedy of the American South* (Baton Rouge, LA: 1979) Louisiana State University Press. Against this backdrop, Hurston wrote and published five of her book-length works.

While Hurston was criticized for focusing on folklore at a time when racialized social oppression was such a major aspect of American life, the material provided in *Mules and Men* and her other writings actually helps to illuminate the everyday ways that black people managed to celebrate life despite the obviously hostile socio-economic climate. A primary cultural context for the folklore and Hoodoo rituals unveiled in *Mules and Men* is the Blues, the oral form that emerged from the everyday coping and survival strategies of southern rural black people. The Blues has been variously defined by such cultural critics as Ralph Ellison and Amiri Baraka. Ellison's often cited definition of the Blues as "an impulse to keep the painful details and episodes of a brutal experience alive in one's aching consciousness, to finger its jagged grain, and to transcend it, not by the consolation of philosophy but by squeezing from it a near-tragic, near comic lyricism," is much narrower in scope than Baraka's. For Baraka, the Blues represents much more than a coping (or chronicling) strategy for former Africans living in a hostile land; it signifies (historically, politically, and socially) African American being, life, and experience.[20] Scholars have traced a Blues voice in African American literature to the colonial era; as a musical form, its origins are connected to the difficult period following the Civil War. The Blues thus evolved as an organic folk form in response to the hard times of the late nineteenth and early twentieth centuries; certainly it captured the mood for the young black men caught up in the Scottsboro saga.

World War II (1939–1945) eventually brought America into full economic recovery. The foundations of World War II were set in place through expansionist moves by several totalitarian regimes led by Adolf Hitler (1889–1945) in Germany, Benito Mussolini (1883–1945) in Italy, and (ultimately) Hideki Tojo (1884–1948) in Japan; Tojo actually became Prime Minister of Japan in October 1941, a short time before the December 7, 1941 Pearl Harbor attack that brought the United States full-scale into the war. Though there were preliminary conflicts dating back to the early 1930s, World War II broke out in earnest in September of 1939 after Nazis invaded Poland, and Britain, France, Australia, and New Zealand declared war on Germany. The following year, President Roosevelt, who was opposed to American involvement, was elected to a precedent-setting third term. By early 1941, however, Congress had approved a program that allowed the president to provide arms and equipment to Great Britain, China, and the Soviet Union, because it deemed those countries vital to America's defense. Also, in response to Japanese aggression in Indochina, the United States froze Japanese assets; Japan demanded release of its assets, a demand countered by the United States' proposal that Japan withdraw from China and Indochina. After requesting two weeks to consider the proposal, the Japanese launched a surprise attack on the US Pacific Fleet at Pearl Harbor on the morning of December 7, 1941. The next day, Congress declared war on Japan, and three days later Germany and Italy declared war on the United States. America's war machine went into overdrive and finally put its capacity for industry to full use, creating jobs, raising money, and increasing investments in education, mining, communications, and trade. The United States' entry into the war ended a period of isolationism but also marked its paranoia in the establishment of "relocation camps" for the internment of Japanese Americans – the majority of whom had been born in the United States and were US citizens – on suspicion of espionage.

World War II had been a test for America as far as many African Americans were concerned. They had served in three major wars and not only were military men still begging for full citizenship rights but they were also being murdered in their uniforms upon returning to the United States. The American military would not be desegregated until 1948 by Executive Order of President Harry S. Truman. In large part because of the continued hostile racial climate of the 1940s and the racism black military men endured at home and abroad, uprisings occurred in several locales during the war, including a major event in Harlem in 1943. According to reports, an African American MP from New Jersey, Private First Class Robert Bandy, hit a white policeman over the head with the policeman's nightstick and was subsequently shot. Bandy was intervening in the white policeman's attempt to arrest a black woman – purportedly for disorderly conduct. The event came on the heels of the murder of a prone black military man by a white policeman in Arkansas. After word reached the African American community that yet another black military man had been shot by a white policeman, blacks and police clashed in a full-scale race riot. The 1943 Harlem riot is re-enacted to some degree in Ralph Ellison's *Invisible Man* (1952).

Though Cold War tensions between the United States and the Soviet Union and their respective allies would begin around 1947 and continue for decades, the period following World War II was a time of prosperity for the United States. Women were encouraged to leave the factory jobs they had taken and return to the domestic sphere and produce children who became part of the "baby-boomer" generation, so called because so many children were born in the decade following the war. Hurston wrote and published *Seraph on the Suwanee* during this time, a novel depicting a prototypical white family achieving the American Dream. (The heroine of Hurston's novel, Arvay Meserve, was also suffering the kind of melancholy then being discussed in the context of Sigmund Freud's work.) African Americans, still subject to Jim Crow rule, yearned to compete fully in the American Dream of economic prosperity and social mobility; by the middle of the 1950s, they had begun a process of organized protest that would ultimately lead to major changes in American society. The process was slow and rife with violence; it marked the final decade of Hurston's life.

In 1955, Chicago, Illinois, teenager Emmett Till was lynched in Money, Mississippi, purportedly for having remarked about the attractiveness of a white woman. The woman's husband and an associate, both of whom had bragged about the murder, were subsequently acquitted by an all-white jury. The same year of Till's murder, long-time NAACP member and activist Rosa Parks (1913–2005) would refuse to move from her seat on a city bus, sparking the Montgomery Bus Boycott; though there had been other boycotts in various places with varying degrees of success, the Montgomery boycott, which lasted over a year and catapulted Martin Luther King, Jr. (1929–1968) to national prominence, is often credited with being the inaugural event of the Civil Rights Movement of the mid-twentieth century. The movement gained a momentum that lasted well into the next decade.

Before Till and Montgomery, the aforementioned 1954 Supreme Court decision in *Brown v. Board of Education of Topeka Kansas* (which challenged segregated public schools) made possible the dismantling of the *Plessy* decision of 1896. Recall that the *Plessy* case made Jim Crow segregation the law of the land; it would take the combined effects of *Brown* and the Civil Rights Act of 1964 to deal the final legal blow to *Plessy*. Hurston was in her early sixties at the time of the *Brown* decision and, in characteristic form, registered her objection in an *Orlando Sentinel* article dated August 11, 1955, "Court Order Can't Make Races Mix." By the end of the 1950s, Martin Luther King, Jr. was a major leader in the blossoming Civil Rights Movement and Malcolm X had risen to a position of prominence in the Nation of Islam, an organization that operated primarily in large urban areas. Malcolm X had become a member while he was imprisoned in Massachusetts. Dwight D. Eisenhower (1890–1969) served two terms as President from 1952 to 1960, and John F. Kennedy was elected President in 1960. Hurston died in 1960 just as America braced for what has come to be known as the most tumultuous decade of the twentieth century. It would be marked by murders, assassinations, and revolutions in the United States and around the globe.

## Notes

1. Keckley (1818–1907) was a formerly enslaved person who wrote an autobiography titled *Behind the Scenes: Or, Thirty Years a Slave, and Four Years in the White House* (New York; G. W. Carleton & Co., 1868).
2. See, Trudier Harris, ed., *Selected Works by Ida B. Wells-Barnett* (New York: Oxford University Press, 1991).
3. Frances Ellen Watkins Harper, *Iola Leroy, or Shadows Uplifted* (1892; College Park, MD: McGrath Publishing, 1969); James Weldon Johnson, *The Autobiography of an Ex-Coloured Man*, 1912; 1927, in *Three Negro Classics*, ed., John Hope Franklin (New York: Avon, 1968), pp. 392–511; Trudier Harris, *Exorcising Blackness: Historical and Literary Lynching and Burning Rituals* (Bloomington, IN: Indiana University Press, 1984).
4. Charles Chesnutt, *The House Behind the Cedars* (1900; Athens, GA: University of Georgia Press, 1988); *The Marrow of Tradition* (1901; New York: Penguin, 1993); Pauline Hopkins, *Contending Forces* (1900; New York and Oxford: Oxford University Press, 1988); Paul Laurence Dunbar, *The Sport of the Gods* (New York: Dodd, Mead & Co., 1902; pt. Miami, FA: Mnemosyne Publishing, 1969).
5. James Baldwin, *Go Tell It on the Mountain* (1953; New York: Laurel-Dell, 1985); *If Beale Street Could Talk* (1974; New York: Dell, 1987); *Tell Me How Long the Train's Been Gone* (New York: Random House, 1968); Toni Morrison, *Beloved* (New York: Knopf, 1987).
6. Booker T. Washington, *Up from Slavery* (1901) ed. William L. Andrews (New York: Norton, 1996.)
7. The oldest HBCU in the United States is Cheyney University of Pennsylvania.
8. The three novels are reprinted as *The Reconstruction Trilogy* (Newport Beach, CA: Noontide Press, 1994).
9. Harriet Beecher Stowe, *Uncle Tom's Cabin* (1852; New York: Garland, 1994).

10. D. W. Griffith, *The Birth of a Nation* (Motion Picture) Reliance-Majestic Studios (1915); Margaret Mitchell, *Gone with the Wind* (1936; New York: Scribner's, 1996); David O. Selznick, *Gone with the Wind* (Motion Picture) Metro Goldwyn Mayer (1939).

11. W. E. B. Du Bois, *The Suppression of the African Slave Trade in America* (1896; New York: Oxford, 2007); *The Souls of Black Folk* (1903; New York: Oxford, 2007).

12. Du Bois would become so disenchanted with American racism that he would move to Ghana in 1961, the year after Hurston died.

13. Historian Deborah Gray White details the movement's activities in *Too Heavy a Load: Black Women in Defense of Themselves* (New York: W. W. Norton, 1999).

14. *Richard Perry Loving, Mildred Jeter Loving v. Virginia*, 388 US 1 (1967).

15. Locke, ed., *The New Negro*, p. xxv.

16. Sutton Griggs, *Imperium in Imperio* (1899) (New York: AMS Press, 1975), p. 62.

17. Locke, ed., *The New Negro*, p. 3.

18. Ibid., p. xxv.

19. Cheryl Wall, *Women of the Harlem Renaissance* (Bloomington, IN: University of Indiana Press, 1995), p. 5.

20. Ralph Ellison, "Richard Wright's Blues" (1945), in *Shadow and Act* (New York: Quality PaperBack Book Club, 1953), pp. 77–94; Amiri Baraka, "The 'Blues Aesthetic' and the 'Black Aesthetic': Aesthetics as the Continuing Political History of a Culture," *Black Music Research Journal* (1991), 101–9. Center for Black Music Research. Columbia College, Chicago, Illinois.

# Works

Politically conservative and staunchly individualist, Zora Neale Hurston often wrote against the grain and suffered the negative criticism of her contemporaries as a result; the choices she made in her professional life reflect the independent spirit that was evident from early childhood, a spirit that made it possible for her to become one of the most published black woman writers of her era. Hurston managed to publish seven books during her lifetime: *Jonah's Gourd Vine* (1934; a novel); *Mules and Men* (1935; folklore); *Their Eyes Were Watching God* (1937; a novel); *Tell My Horse* (1938; folklore); *Moses, Man of the Mountain* (1939; a novel); *Dust Tracks on a Road* (1942; autobiography); and *Seraph on the Suwanee* (1948; a novel). All volumes except *Seraph on the Suwanee* were published by J. B. Lippincott. Hurston never produced a contracted second volume of her autobiography; however, she wrote and/or produced scores of shorter works, including short stories, plays, and essays. Hurston's seven book-length works and some of her most often anthologized short stories are examined below.

## *Jonah's Gourd Vine* (1934; a novel)

### *Time period and setting*

The action of *Jonah's Gourd Vine* proceeds from around 1880 through the first decades of the twentieth century as we follow John Buddy Pearson from his tenant-farmer adolescence through his courtship and marriage to Lucy Ann Potts, his many infidelities, and his two subsequent marriages. The time period covers roughly forty-five years. Hurston sets the story primarily in the town of her birth, Notasulga, Alabama, and in and around the town she called home, Eatonville, Florida. The Big Creek (the Songahatchee River) separates Notasulga into two areas, one more rural in character than the other. The title character, John Pearson, grows up on the poorer side of the creek but crosses to the other side where he first meets Lucy. For a short time, John joins a work camp on the Alabama River and, during the early years of his marriage to Lucy, flees to the Sanford-Eatonville area to avoid a court date. Eatonville eventually becomes the family's home, and some of John's extramarital infidelities take place in a nearby town called Oviedo; his last official residence is Plant City, Florida, with third wife Sally Lovelace.

## Major characters

John Buddy Pearson is the teenage son of twentysomething Amy Crittenden and Alf Pearson, the white man who owned Amy when slavery was legal in the United States. Two of John Buddy's five brothers, Zeke and Zachariah, are mentioned by name and appear several times in the story. Though John bears the Crittenden name at the beginning of the story, he takes the name Pearson after crossing over the Songahatchee River. Essentially fatherless, John's major flaw is a lack of self-knowledge, obviously related to questions surrounding his parentage. In typical *Bildungsroman* format, the narrative tracks his journey toward self-knowledge. He becomes a successful carpenter and, most significantly, a poet/preacher whose capacity for language makes him one of the most respected preachers in the region. John's relationships with women are central to his journey. From his exemplary mother, Amy, he acquires an enterprising attitude and a magical way with words. Through his many easy sexual encounters, he develops a false sense of phallic power. His relationship with wife Lucy continues to some degree the maternal relationship, for Lucy teaches him, nurtures him, and grooms him to be the successful provider he becomes; she is a major (though increasingly unappreciated) source of his strength and power. Hattie Tyson uses conjure to displace Lucy; however, she lacks the qualities in a life-partner that the seriously flawed John requires. The relationship with Hattie leads to his decline. John meets Sally Lovelace when he is effectively wandering in exile. She offers him the shelter of her arms and her substantial property. She also sends him back to Eatonville in a new Cadillac, the car in which he's riding when he collides with a locomotive.

Steady and resilient, Amy Crittenden is a practical woman, a formerly enslaved person, who tries to make the best hand of the cards she has been dealt in life. Hurston might say that Amy tries to "hit a straight lick with a crooked stick." Twentysomething Amy is the mother of six sons, the oldest (John Buddy) having been born in slavery during or before Amy's twelfth year. Recognizing how difficult it was for slave parents to bond properly with their offspring, Amy loves, nurtures, and tries to protect her children. Just as she negotiates the narrow socio-economic parameters of her existence, she will not accept passively her bitter husband's abuses and attempted abuses to her and her children. In her physical battles with him, she is usually able to hold her own. When Amy learns that Ned has bound John to a notoriously cruel planter named Mimms, she sends John across the Big Creek with her blessing and with the advice that he look up Alf Pearson. She is neither bitter nor self-serving as she goes about the routines of her difficult tenant-farming life. Despite Amy's limited presence in the novel, her capacity for action and language become her legacy to John Buddy and thus make her an essential character in the story of John's life.

Amy's husband and John's stepfather, Ned Crittenden, is a bitter and emasculated middle-aged tenant farmer who lacks the self-confidence it would take to conceive of a plan for moving his family beyond its impoverished conditions. Physically and psychologically abusive to his wife and children – and especially disdainful of stepson John Buddy – Ned is both fearful and envious of white maleness and white male privilege. While Amy suggests that Ned had at first welcomed her half-white son, the teenage John Buddy eventually became a physical reminder of the white man's dominance over his life. The basic differences between Amy's and Ned's responses to slavery and the socio-economic trap of tenant farming are psychological and (to some degree) gender-related. In addition to working alongside Ned in the fields, Amy must care for a husband and six sons, and yet she manages to avoid (or perhaps she cannot afford) the self-destructive bitterness that clearly consumes Ned and thus keeps him spiritually and psychologically enslaved. Hurston's personal philosophy and her politics of self-determination and personal responsibility are visible in her portrayal of Ned as someone whose slave mentality serves as a major impediment to his psychological and economic well-being. His psychologically enslaved prototype will show up in a collective sense among the newly freed Hebrews of Hurston's third novel, *Moses, Man of the Mountain.*

Lucy Ann Potts, whose family believes strongly in the value of education, is the brightest student in John Buddy's classes at school. Possessed of a willful nature and a strong character, Lucy is several years younger than John and petite in stature. She teaches John from their school books, enhancing and formalizing the capacity for language that John inherits from his mother. John recognizes in Lucy a better version of himself, and she becomes the love of his life. Perhaps Lucy sees in John an outlet for her obvious substantial capacity for nurturing; she eventually marries him against the wishes of her parents, and (barred from the Potts family property) their first home is in the quarters on Alf Pearson's plantation. Lucy maintains the best possible home for her family, bears John several children, and serves as his loyal and intelligent helpmate – consistently trying to guide him toward an ideal of manhood. After the family moves to Eatonville, she nurtures him toward successful careers in carpentering and preaching. Despite his constant philandering, Lucy remains steadfastly loyal, and the family continues to prosper while she is alive.

Lucy's death creates a moral vacuum for John, who soon marries Hattie Tyson – a woman as self-centered and conniving as Lucy had been generous and straightforward. The narrative suggests that Lucy's illness and death, and John's decision to marry Hattie only three months after Lucy's death, were facilitated by a Hoodoo fix that Hattie solicited. Hattie is more possessive than loving; like John, she allows her libido too much sway over her life, and both she and John engage in numerous extramarital sexual encounters. They bring out the worst in each other and their volatile relationship poisons the atmosphere in the previously comforting home environment that Lucy had created.

Richard and Emmeline Potts are Lucy's proud, property-owning middle-class-valued parents. Though they had, like the Crittendens, been born in slavery, they have managed to acquire and hold on to substantial property. They want Lucy to marry well and continue their family's ascent, and thus discourage her relationship with dirt-poor John Buddy. They are sorely disappointed when Lucy chooses to marry him, anyway; Emmeline refuses to attend the wedding and subsequently bars her daughter from the family home, effectively disinheriting her.

Former slaveholder Alf Pearson has converted his antebellum plantation to a profitable tenant-farming system. He recognizes himself in the strapping mulatto youth (John Buddy) who comes to him seeking employment; however, to avoid the obvious question of parentage he immediately lies to a white friend that John Buddy was born *after* slavery. We learn from the narrative that Amy was around 12 when the Civil War ended, so Alf Pearson would have impregnated her before she reached her teens. Pearson still rules over the lives of his black workers and servants, reveling in all the entitlements and privileges of being propertied, white, and male in the late nineteenth-century American south. John's rooster status among the young women who live and work on the Pearson plantation is amusing to Alf and reminds him of his own youthful sexual exploits among his female property. Alf sends John Buddy to school, provides some material support, offers him sound advice about women and marriage, and ends up saving him from the chain gang. Careful readers will note that Alf serves as an interesting counterpoint to Ned Crittenden. Surface readers are much more inclined to *like* the former slaveholder/pedophile Alf than they are the impoverished, emasculated, and psychologically enslaved Ned.

Hambo and Harris are Deacons at Zion Hope Church. Two-faced and envious, Harris smiles in John's face while joining forces with Hattie and others against him; Hambo remains John's loyal and faithful friend from beginning to end. He warns John about the growing tide against him. When John returns to Eatonville for the last time before he is killed, he stays with his friend Hambo. John's third and last wife, Sally Lovelace, is a good woman, a widow, who owns some thirty houses. She meets John when he is down on his luck after he has divorced Hattie and walked away from his position at Zion Hope. Self-assured and patient, she provides the stability John needs at that point in his life. A modified version of Lucy, Sally is a strong and protective presence and a good match for John. She knows how to help him without emasculating him; she provides the nurturing kind of support from a partner that John clearly requires in order to live up to his potential. The narrative suggests that in order to become his best self, John requires the partnership of a woman of a certain character, women like Lucy and Sally. As Shakespeare would suggest through his work, certain types are complementary and complimentary when merged, while others can be volatile and lethal (as in the case of Hattie and John). While Sally seems to be the best possible partner for John at that point in his life, it was Sally who bought him the new Cadillac and convinced him to go back to Eatonville and show it off. Her suggestion resulted indirectly in his death, and we have to remember that she was a widow when John met her.

## The surface story

The story begins at dinnertime in the Crittenden family cabin on the poorer side of the Big Creek. A rainstorm has driven the family indoors where Amy prepares the meal. Ned Crittenden displays his irate nature and lack of character by verbally attacking first Amy and then John. Ned voices his resentment of light-skinned John Buddy in a way that suggests it is an ongoing refrain in the household. He and Amy argue after Ned reveals his plan to bind John over to Cap'n Mimms, a former overseer known for his cruelty and brutality. Angered by his inability to get the best of Amy, Ned later attacks her with a whip; when she threatens to get the best of him in the ensuing battle, he chokes her.

John Buddy intervenes on his mother's behalf, an act that further angers Ned who wants John (the physical reminder of white male dominance) out of his presence one way or the other. Amy's response is to send John across the Songahatchee; she tells him to go to Alf Pearson for assistance. Along the way to the Pearson plantation, John meets and engages in dialogue with 11-year-old Lucy Ann Potts.

As it happens, John's maternal grandmother, Pheemy, still lives and works on the Pearson plantation; John shares her living quarters. He also receives some of Alfred Junior's castoff clothing. Pearson's legitimate son is conveniently away, studying abroad. Though John is large and strapping, Pearson puts him to work performing relatively easy tasks that include feeding chickens, collecting eggs, providing surveillance on Pearson's other black workers, and keeping a count of Pearson's farm animals in an effort to thwart thefts.

John quickly attracts the attention of several female adolescents who compete (with some success) for his attentions; however, when he begins school, he becomes quite taken with Lucy Potts and reserves his serious attention for her. Lucy is only 12, however, and – according to her mother – four years younger than she needs to be to keep male company. Still, John lets Lucy know how much he thinks of her. Despite their obvious economic class differences and Lucy's mother's objections, the two manage to spend time together. However, when the Crittenden family takes up tenant farming at a different plantation and the owner insists that John Buddy be part of the package, Amy travels across the creek to retrieve John. John rejoins his family, but a final confrontation with Ned (whom he describes as a "burnt off trunk of a tree") results in his return to the Pearson plantation and the continuation of his relationship with Lucy. John joins Lucy's church, and they both sing in the choir. Their love is in full bloom, though they are forced to keep the fact of their relationship a secret from Lucy's parents.

Meanwhile, John (though he clearly wants Lucy to be his wife someday) continues to give his libido free rein among the young women on the Pearson place. John finds work at a tie-camp on the Alabama River after he is forced to leave Notasulga abruptly to avoid a violent encounter after another man's woman expresses her desire for him. Women continue to make themselves available to John and he willingly obliges them even as he keeps Lucy in his plans for the future. He remains with the tie-camp until his brother Zeke delivers a letter from Lucy; they both return to Notasulga at Christmastime, and John presents Lucy with a huge china doll as a present. Lucy's mother is highly upset by what the gift represents and tells Lucy that she is promised to Artie Mimms (who, significantly, bears the same last name as the white planter to whom Ned had earlier attempted to bind John). Like Logan Killicks of *Their Eyes*

*Were Watching God*, Mimms is an older man who owns substantial property. A willful Lucy continues to see John and eventually they are allowed a limited public courtship; nevertheless, when they finally marry, Lucy's mother refuses to attend the ceremony.

Alf Pearson gives Lucy and John a walnut bed as a wedding present, and they set up housekeeping on the Pearson place in the servants' quarters. John recognizes the value of Lucy as a wife; yet, he continues to have sexual relations with a woman named Mehaley until she marries and moves away. He also cheats on Lucy with Big 'Oman, and almost drowns returning from a rendezvous with her. He learns that Lucy knows about his seemingly never-ending string of infidelities, but he continues to indulge his libido. John is clearly not living up to his potential, and his family is suffering economically. While Lucy is giving birth to their fourth child, and there is no food in the house, John is away with a woman named Delphine. Lucy's brother comes to collect a debt while Lucy is still in bed from having given birth and takes the only real item of value: the bed that had been Alf Pearson's wedding present to them. John finally returns home, locates Lucy's brother, and beats the man badly. He also steals and kills a pig to provide food for his family. Arrested for both offenses, he takes Alf Pearson's advice and puts distance between himself and Notasulga after Pearson (who is, as it happens, also the judge) arranges for him to be released in his charge. Always fascinated by trains (to which many ascribe phallic symbolism), John takes his first train ride to Sanford, Florida, and finds work on a railroad. He sends his extra money home to Lucy and sets about experiencing the good and the bad of railroad work. After attending a church service, John apes the preacher to much praise. He learns about the nearby all-black town of Eatonville and goes there to work in Sam Mosely's orchards. Almost a year passes before he finally sends for his family.

Lucy approves of Eatonville as a choice, her life as the child of property-owning black people having taught her the importance of not living daily life in the immediate shadow of white supremacy. She continues to exemplify the attributes of the proper wife; she is supportive and strong, gently guiding her husband in the right direction with careful attention to his fragile manhood. She encourages him to use his carpentering skills, and he prospers. She encourages him to preach, and he soon becomes the most sought after preacher in the region. Eventually, he ascends to the pastorship of Zion Hope Church in Eatonville, and he also runs successfully for mayor against his former employer, Sam Mosely. Despite all his social and economic successes, a loving wife, and a growing family, however, John continues to be unfaithful to Lucy. The church takes note and when Deacon Harris makes John aware of their distaste for his indiscretions, he preaches a special sermon about natural men that wins the congregation's hearts and minds. He is able to keep his church, and his wife remains steadfastly loyal.

John's undoing comes after Lucy becomes ill and dies. As a final insult to Lucy, he capped off his many infidelities by slapping her as she lay dying. The story suggests that John's irrational act is a result of a Hoodoo fix; he has come under the influence of conjure, for Hattie has been using the services of An' Dangie Dewoe, a conjure woman. Hattie believes that the circumstances leading to her victory over Lucy Potts are the result of the conjure woman's services. John's family and community frown on his decision to marry Hattie only three months after Lucy's death. In character, Hattie bears little resemblance to Lucy and, under the much younger but more conniving woman's spell, John's fortunes change for the worse. Ultimately, his children are either forced out or leave of their own accord. Without Lucy's gentle and intelligent guidance and support, John falters, and his marriage to Hattie deteriorates. Both partners rack up numerous infidelities. John, a man who had – prior to having slapped Lucy on her deathbed – considered it useless to hit a woman, begins to beat Hattie. Later, he cannot seem to remember why he married her. When he discovers that Hattie had used Hoodoo to manipulate him, he beats her very badly; Hattie leaves and sues for a divorce – which John (nearing 60 years of age) does not contest.

The same Deacon Harris who had warned John years before that the congregation was turning against him joins forces with Hattie to have John ousted as Zion Hope's pastor. When Hattie tries to bring charges of adultery against John, however, Hambo reminds everyone that the two are divorced and, thus, Hattie has no standing to charge him with infidelity. Understanding that the congregation has largely turned against him, John, whose word-wizardry is by then legendary, preaches an earth-shattering sermon and voluntarily leaves the pulpit and the church. He cannot reconcile his biological sexual urges with the protocol for a proper minister and husband. Once he abdicates his position as pastor, his carpentering business falters. Shunned and looking for work, he leaves the Sanford-Eatonville area and ends up in Plant City, Florida, where he meets the woman who becomes his third wife: Sally Lovelace. Having spent much time in introspection, John seems a changed man; he remembers Lucy and reflects on their years together. He tries to understand how he squandered such a good and valuable resource.

His new wife, Sally, is also a valuable resource; indeed, she is a modified, more independent version of Lucy. Sally owns substantial property that needs care, so once again good fortune shines on John by bestowing him with a strong, supportive wife, a wonderful home, and economic security. When Sally presents him with a new Cadillac and urges him to travel back to Eatonville to show off his prosperity, he cannot resist. He spends several days visiting his friend Hambo while trying to ignore the advances of younger women who are drawn to John and his shiny new car. John gives in to one final dalliance in a dingy room in Oviedo with a voluptuous young woman named Ora, but he is almost immediately ashamed of his weakness. Driving home to the woman he now realizes is his second real chance at a good life, finally understanding the value of what he has, he is struck by a train and killed. He is widely mourned.

## Analysis

*Jonah's Gourd Vine* is autobiographical in that it revisits the relationship between Hurston's own mother and father. Hurston changes her father's last name to Pearson in the novel; however, she changes neither first nor last names for her mother Lucy Ann Potts, nor for Lucy's parents, Richard and Emmeline. Hurston's autobiography and the biographies of her life reveal that many of the situations, settings, and events depicted in the novel are factual.

The title *Jonah's Gourd Vine* refers to the biblical story of Jonah, specifically Jonah 4:6–10, a parable about a gourd vine that grows to huge proportions overnight only to be destroyed by a worm. So the story goes, God made the gourd vine grow in order to provide shade/shelter for Jonah. Collectively, Lucy, home, family, and community serve as the most obvious parallel to the sheltering vine – though Lucy clearly represents the core or central aspect of it. The obvious parallel to the destructive worm is John's unbridled libido, which results in the collapse of the shelter's foundation. John's sexual liaison with Hattie leads Hattie to seek power over Lucy through conjure, which results in Lucy's illness and death. The story offers a warning about the destruction that can result from lack of self-knowledge and awareness, John Buddy Pearson's lack of awareness being manifested most obviously in the problematic expression of his manhood and in his inability to appreciate the value of his sheltering vine.

Hurston accomplishes several objectives in the two opening chapters of the novel, while advancing the central plot of John's journey toward self-discovery. First of all, she uses the Crittenden household to expose readers to the interior lives of a typical tenant-farming family. While the tenant-farming lifestyle represented a culminating socio-economic dynamic between uneducated, socially circumscribed, property-less families, and planters who still owned plenty of property, Hurston reveals a family nevertheless engaged in their daily routines of working, playing, dining, and so on. By the end of the first chapter, we are well aware of Ned Crittenden's bitterness, Amy Crittenden's strong maternal instincts, and John Buddy Pearson's uniqueness.

Hurston also inserts into the early chapters the topic of sexual exploitation of black women under slavery and black female sexuality in general. We not only learn, for example, that John Buddy is the son of his mother's former owner, Alfred Pearson, but also that Amy had given birth to the child before she entered her teens. Hurston takes care to separate the two passages that, taken together, reveal this information. In a very early passage about Robert E. Lee's surrender, Amy recalls that she was only 12 when Lee surrendered in April of 1865. Later, when John arrives at the Pearson plantation, Alf Pearson lies to cover up the fact that he had fathered John during slavery. Taken together, the two passages reveal that Amy was probably under 12 when Alf Pearson began having sex with her. At Pearson's plantation, John enjoys the role of plantation rooster among adolescent girls and young women while he waits for Lucy to come of age. The major difference between John's rooster status and that enjoyed by Alf Pearson under slavery is that John possesses and exercises no power or control over the lives of his sex partners other than what they allow him. Nor does John seek a sexual outlet in barely pubescent children as Alf Pearson obviously had done in the case of John's mother, Amy. Alf Pearson's unusual post-slavery interventions into the sex lives of his black employees (even providing John and Lucy's marital bed) reveals an intrusive paternalism that has continued far beyond the official end of slavery.

Echoing one of her major political and philosophical influences, Booker T. Washington, Hurston also makes formal education and the acquisition and application of knowledge in general central to the novel by pointing to the importance of education and to the difference that education could make in the lives of the formerly enslaved and their descendants. Washington's philosophy of personal responsibility and self-determination is manifested thematically throughout the narrative in John's personal story and in the background story of Eatonville. When John first meets Lucy, it is within the context of the schoolyard from which he has previously been literally fenced out as a member of a tenant-farming family forced to work while others attend school. Much of their courtship unfolds in and around the schoolhouse, making it even more significant that John's association with his white father provides the opportunity for him to attend school. John Buddy's life is to some extent an application of the formula for black progress that Washington articulates in his 1895 Atlanta Exposition Speech. Additionally, the real-life Lucy Potts worked briefly as a country schoolteacher, and Hurston grew up in a household where her mother made education central to her children's everyday lives. Thus, the focus on education in the novel is no accident; rather, it is a deliberate strategy to underscore the relationship between education and black self-empowerment.

Hurston also makes readers aware of the socio-economic distinctions between John – the illegitimate black son – and Alfred, Jr. – the legitimate white heir. Alfred, Jr. is studying abroad and will reap the benefits and privileges that come with an expensive college education. After spending most of his adolescent years laboring in tenant-farming and other forms of manual labor, John will have to draw on his basic education and natural talents to prosper. When John Buddy arrives at Alfred Pearson's plantation looking for work, he is, ironically, returning to the place of his mother's and his own former enslavement. He is, along with numerous others, a neo-slave. On either side of the Big Creek, black Americans continued to live under white rule and were subject to economic exploitation. Amy's mother, Pheemy, is still a servant on the plantation where John had been born, and John's "reunion" with his grandmother is represented in a way that speaks volumes about the disruptive effects slavery had on intimate family relationships. Again, the careful reader will connect Amy's chapter 1 comments about how slavery interfered with the proper nurturance of children with the manner in which John is introduced to his grandmother in chapter 2.

Having already established the socio-economic differential and the interdependent character of the relationship between Pearson and his tenants, Hurston broaches the issue of theft. Theft becomes a significant issue wherever there are rigid socio-economic divisions among people living in close proximity to one another. Alf places John in charge of surveillance over the other black workers; in particular, he is to keep an accurate count of the number of pigs being born so as to discourage thefts by other workers. The second time John leaves Pearson's plantation, Pearson – whose abundant resources are the result of his exploitation of black labor – admonishes him not to steal. Hurston's references to theft here and elsewhere in her writing suggest she is well aware of the stereotype of the black thief that emerged from America's skewed socio-economic history, and which had been treated to some extent in the work of her black literary predecessors. Hurston, who has written about learning that she was not standard upon leaving Eatonville, made the white characters in her novel standard by failing to designate their racial affiliation as she did her black characters. Like Washington, she was skillful enough to skirt overt social protest even as she included information that could be read, considered, and interpreted from a variety of perspectives. The idea that property matters is highlighted throughout the novel, from the property-less Crittenden family to the property-wealthy Alf Pearson and the middle-class property-owning Potts family. Later, John Pearson realizes his own dream of property ownership, loses it, and then acquires more property through marriage. One leaves the novel with an understanding of how much property mattered (whether it was the two bales of cotton that would have made all the difference to the tenant-farming Crittendens, or the fine Eatonville home John eventually built for his family) to the descendants of people who had once themselves been considered property.

For John Buddy Pearson, property was clearly not enough; while he emerges as a strong, attractive, gifted, and intelligent man – a poet in the style of the best southern rural black preachers – his inability to control his libido leads him into the relationship with Hattie Tyson that culminates in Lucy's death and John's subsequent alienation from family, church, and community.[1] Though John recognized the special qualities of Lucy's womanhood and married her because of them, he continued to be libido-driven and, as one of his church sermons illustrates, believes that he is only doing what a natural man should do. His fragile sense of self depends too much on phallic power, and his life ends on a tragic note, ironically during a moment of deep introspection when he finally seems to have achieved the wisdom that would allow him to appreciate his new sheltering vine.

Because Hurston has previously made much of John's fascination with the physicality of trains – from the awe of seeing his first locomotive, to his amazing first train ride – John's failure to notice the train in his path speaks volumes about the degree to which he was preoccupied with self-reflection during the final moments of his life. The vision of John Buddy's first encounter with a train and the obvious connection of that train with masculine power and aggressiveness returns, with the ultimate symbol of phallic energy and power causing John's death. With John's life so closely paralleling that of Hurston's own father, the character's state of mind at novel's end perhaps suggests the author's desire that her father achieved self-knowledge before his own tragic death.

## Mules and Men (1935)

### Time period and setting

Hurston conducted the research for *Mules and Men* between 1927 and 1932, though she completed much of the actual collecting of tales and rituals by 1930. Serving as the volume's semi-fictional narrator and mediator of the tales, songs, and rituals collected therein, Hurston collapses the time period for her several expeditions into one collective expedition of less than two years. While Hurston collected tales in and around Eatonville, Florida, at a sawmill camp near Loughman, Florida, and at a phosphate mining camp in Pierce, Florida, she traveled to Louisiana (and New Orleans, in particular) to collect material for part two ("Hoodoo") of the volume. The Hoodoo section focuses on Hurston's interactions with the conjurers and/or Hoodoo doctors whose names appear in the table of contents. Hoodoo cannot be constrained to time or place. Though a number of the folk tales, particularly the "John" stories, are set during slavery, most are fluid and (likewise) timeless, easily adapted and updated.

## Major characters

As facilitator/mediator, Hurston is the central character in this collection. Each location features a different atmosphere and a different cast of supporting characters who serve as audience and/or provide the lore. In Eatonville, these include George Thomas, Calvin Daniels, Jack and Charlie Jones, Gene Brazzle, B. Moseley, Mayor Hiram Lester, Gene and Gold (husband and wife), and Mathilda Moseley. When Hurston travels south to Polk County and the Everglades Cypress Lumber Company camp near Loughman, Florida, she interacts with a new group, including Joe Willard, Slim, James Presley, a traveling preacher (who delivers an apt sermon "Behold de Rib"), Nunkie, Ella Wall, Lucy, and the all important Big Sweet; Big Sweet intervenes to save Hurston when a jealous Lucy tries to attack her with a knife in a jook joint. Around Mulberry, Pierce, and Lakeland, Florida, she encounters Mack C. Ford, Good Bread, Christopher Jenkins, Mah Honey, Horace Sharp, and others. When Zora travels further south to New Orleans to explore Hoodoo, she engages with the spirit of Marie Leveau, deemed to have been the greatest Hoodoo teacher of them all. That experience is mediated by Luke Turner, who claims to be Leveau's nephew. Hurston interacts with a number of other people, including the following Hoodoo experts: Eulalia; Anatol Pierre; Father Watson; Dr. Duke; and Kitty Brown.

## Format and contents

Hurston dedicated *Mules and Men* to Annie Nathan Meyer, the Barnard founder who helped her gain admission to the college. Columbia University anthropologist Franz Boas wrote the volume's preface. Hurston wrote an introduction to the volume that begins with the often repeated statement, "I was glad when somebody told me, 'You may go and collect Negro folk-lore.'" The volume's contents are divided into two primary parts, "Folk Tales" and "Hoodoo." Hurston's position as narrator/mediator allows her to provide contexts for tales, songs, and rituals, and also to illustrate performative aspects of each entry. Part one contains seventy tales and parts of tales; it is further divided into ten subparts that group tales together based on common social context, location, or subject matter. Part two contains seven subparts that include conjure stories, information about the origins of Hoodoo, and details about rituals learned under several conjurers and/or Hoodoo doctors. The rituals are typically geared toward specific objectives such as ruling the man you love, keeping a husband faithful, and exerting power over your enemies and perceived enemies. A glossary and an appendix containing four sections – "Negro Songs with Music," "Formulae of Hoodoo Doctors," "Paraphernalia of Conjure," and "Prescriptions of Root Doctors" – round out the volume.

The folk tales collected in *Mules and Men* are like much of African American folklore in terms of form and function. What makes the volume unique is Hurston's approach and form of mediation; her participatory approach allows her to become part of the group under study. The result is a rich and multidimensional collection unlike anything that had been produced before, for it is within the contexts of the exchanges and conversations among the group, and between members of the group and Hurston as narrator, that the true meaning of each tale is revealed without the intrusion of scholarly analysis. The volume unfolds like a novel, complete with plot, antagonists, protagonists, and recurring themes and motifs, rather than a scientific classification of information that further subjugates the people under study.

Part one features sermons, songs, and several kinds of tales, including tall tales such as "The Goat that Flagged a Train" and "Tall Hunting Story," and origin tales such as "How the Cat Got Nine Lives" and "How the Squinch Owl Came to Be." The tales that most often reflect awareness of oppression and the will to survive under oppression are the trickster tales. Trickster tales involving animals typically feature physically small or weak animals consistently outwitting physically superior animals. Tricksters are not, however, necessarily moral figures; in fact, they typically ignore rules and laws in their insistence on simply having what they want by any means necessary. Sometimes, they are themselves tricked through their own work. For example, the story Hurston includes in subpart six of "Folk Tales," "How Brer Dog Lost His Beautiful Voice," features a competition between a dog and a rabbit in the courtship of a maiden. As the smaller, weaker creature, the rabbit's task becomes that of destroying the dog's beautiful singing voice. He does so by splitting the dog's tongue; however, from that point on the dog chases the rabbit who can ill afford to stop at the home of the object of his affection for fear of being caught. One of the most famous and enduring human trickster figures is John, also referred to as John the Conquerer or High John the Conquerer (a term that also describes a specific root used in conjuring). Such tales often come packaged as "John and Massa" stories and feature John as an heroic slave outwitting his master.

Examples from the volume include "Ole Massa and John Who Wanted to Go to Heaven," "Massa and the Bear," and "Deer Hunting Story." Such were the tales employed by backwoods Floridians as coping devices for the socio-economic oppressions they faced in their everyday lives.

If one pays careful attention to the movement of Hurston's text, from Eatonville where women's voices are dominated and the tales – most often given voice by men – cast women in unfavorable and/or inferior light, to the New Orleans area where no particular value is attached to gender among Hoodoo doctors and conjurers, a much more specific objective becomes apparent. Hurston uses *Mules and Men* to demonstrate that the greater the distance from the pre-Christian, Afrocentric system of belief represented via Hoodoo, the more narrow the vision women have of themselves and their lives. In Eatonville, men routinely give voice to unflattering and sexist stories and comments about the nature of women; on the rare occasion that a woman is allowed to speak at length, her story does nothing to undermine sexist and unflattering representations of women. For example, Mathilda Moseley's tale, "Why Women Always Take Advantage of Men," begins with men and women as equals until God grants the man his request for more strength. Being turned down by God for a similar request, the woman must obtain her power from Satan. Female subjectivity and power are thus associated with the ultimate symbol of evil.

Moving away from Eatonville, Zora encounters Big Sweet and the lumber camp community. Big Sweet serves as an alternative to standard representations of women as weak or inferior; indeed, she defies gender expectations. She is widely respected (and sometimes feared) by men and women alike, and the fact that she will not allow her voice to be subjugated to those of men means that she recognizes herself as a subject and actor in the world. She is second to no one, even the white quarters boss she stands up to in one episode; her significance is sealed when she saves Zora's life. Her story and the episodes involving her are well positioned to follow the Eatonville episodes in "Folktales" and lead up to "Hoodoo." Structuring the volume in this way allows for a reading that takes the reader from the rigidly gendered space of Eatonville and the androgynous adventures of Big Sweet, to the realm of Hoodoo where the genders are balanced in terms of power and where the most revered and powerful of all Hoodoo doctors is a woman who has been dead for decades.

Much of the material in "Hoodoo" had been published in 1931 as "Hoodoo in America" in the *Journal of American Folklore*, though Hurston changed some of the names of the Hoodoo doctors for *Mules and Men*. She begins part two with a rationale for traveling to what she deemed the Hoodoo capital of America, New Orleans. Nobody knows how Hoodoo started, she tells us, but it "started way back there before everything. Six days of magic spells and mighty words and the world with its elements above and below was made. And now, God is leaning back taking a seventh day rest."[2] In other words, Hoodoo preceded the universe's creation and thus the Creator of the universe was the first Hoodoo doctor; the biblical Moses (after whom she fashioned the title character of *Moses, Man of the Mountain*) was also a great Hoodoo doctor, his greatest feat being to secure the release of the Hebrews from slavery and lead them to the site of the Promised Land.

"Hoodoo," Hurston explained in "Hoodoo in America," "is a term related to the West African term '*juju*.'" Among African Americans, the term is also used interchangeably with "conjure" and "roots," though these two terms are more readily associated with healing, rather than magic. Hurston biographer Robert Hemenway offers a straightforward definition of the collective terms "Hoodoo" and "conjure" as standing for "all the traditional beliefs in black culture centering around a votary's confidence in the power of a conjure, root, two-head, or Hoodoo doctor to alter with magical powers a situation that seems rationally irremediable." Hemenway notes importantly that "Conjure has historically provided an access to power for a powerless people, and many of its traditions are ancient. It is an alternative mode for perceiving reality, contrasting sharply with what is perceived as the white man's excessive rationality."[3] Hurston notes also that because Hoodoo was not widely accepted, believers often concealed their faith. One became a Hoodoo doctor through inheritance, by apprenticeship, or calling.

The next section recounts Hurston's experiences with six conjurers: Eulalia; Luke Turner; Anatol Pierre; Father Watson; Dr. Duke; and Kitty Brown. Except in the subpart covering her time with Eulalia, Hurston relates information about rituals, curses, and/or ceremonies obtained from each engagement. Collectively, the information reveals that Hoodoo serves a number of purposes, including healing, empowerment over real or perceived adversaries of varying kinds (including causing the adversary's death), and securing love or the loyalty of a loved one. Some conjurers and root doctors focus only on healing, while others engage in other work requiring *magic*. All practices are typically categorized as Hoodoo, though there is some slippage. Hurston also provides background information on Marie Leveau, a third-generation Hoodoo queen whose spirit still presided over the New Orleans Hoodoo world Hurston visited in the 1920s though Leveau had been born around 1827 and died around the turn of the twentieth century. Hurston was able to apprentice with Leveau's grand-nephew Luke Turner (whom she calls Samuel Thompson in "Hoodoo in America") after proving her devotion by lying for over sixty hours face down and nude, without food and water.

For Hurston, the men and women who become Hoodoo doctors and are deemed irrational and superstitious by most people are in reality and actuality demonstrating a profound understanding of many natural secrets. A wonderful example of such understanding informs her depiction of Moses' ability to cross the Red Sea at a particular point and a particular time when he knew the water would recede sufficiently. That Hurston was a true believer is evident in her own statement that people "really can do things to you." In *Mules and Men*, "Hoodoo" provides an appropriate complement to "Folktales," for it serves as a more tangible resource for illustrating how oppressed and subjugated persons coped with the challenging realities of their everyday lives. One might say that it is the organic material from which the folktales emerge. Along with *Tell My Horse*, *Mules and Men* serves as the source for much of the folklore Hurston incorporates into her short stories and novels.

## *Their Eyes Were Watching God* (1937)

### Time period and setting

Hurston wrote *Their Eyes Were Watching God* in 1936 while she was conducting research on Voodoo in Haiti for *Tell My Horse*; her construction of the novel's protagonist reveals the influence of her research, for one sees in Janie Crawford a combination of two female Voodoo deities.[4] The novel's narrative begins with Janie's return to Eatonville, Florida, in the 1920s. She tells her friend Phoeby the story of her life, a life that had begun some forty years earlier in West Florida. Though her reflections about part of her mother's and grandmother's lives extend the time period back to the beginning of the Civil War and other locales, most of the story unfolds in the early twentieth century in Eatonville, Florida, an actual town located some ten miles northeast of Orlando, Florida. We follow teenage Janie from the West Florida home of her grandmother to her first marital home in the same general area, on to Eatonville with her second husband, and further south to the Everglades – specifically Belle Glade – and marriage to her third husband. In the end Janie returns home to Eatonville, though the most dramatic aspects of her transformation take place in Belle Glade.

### Major characters

Janie Mae Crawford Killicks Starks Woods is the protagonist, and the account of her journey toward self-actualization comprises the narrative; born Janie Mae Crawford, she is described as extremely attractive, with very light skin and long black hair. Janie is a mulatto child born of rape; her mother Leafy had been born of an exploitative relationship between master and slave. Janie must find a way to move beyond the problematic sexual legacy that has been passed down to her through her mother's and her grandmother's experiences even as she dreams of romance and adventure, of experiencing sexual fulfillment with a man she loves, and of seeking the Horizon (a metaphor for exploring life to the fullest). Janie wants to express herself in a way that feels natural and organic; to do so, she must resist others' attempts to usurp her own vision for her life. Though her first two marriages end in failure, she learns something valuable about herself from each of them so that by the time she meets the love of her life she is able to express her natural, organic self with confidence.

Phoeby Watson is Janie's best friend in Eatonville. Phoeby is loyal, intelligent, and unassuming; over the years, she had proven herself to be Janie's good friend. When Janie returns to Eatonville, and the community is quick to sit in judgment of her, Phoeby refuses to join them; rather, she decides to deliver her friend a meal and receive Janie's story first hand. Thus, she offers the unbiased ear that hears the story Janie narrates.

Nanny Crawford is Janie's grandmother; a formerly enslaved woman who had been sexually exploited by her white owner, Nanny took on the responsibility for Janie's rearing after Janie's mother Leafy disappeared. Nanny is, above all, practical and wants her granddaughter to have a good, easy life. When she realizes that teenage Janie is experiencing her sexual awakening, she quickly marries her off to a much older man of property. Nanny sees in the marriage the potential for Janie to have both the protection and the respectability that neither she nor her disgraced daughter enjoyed. Nanny's limited perception of Janie's options is based on her own circumscribed life experiences and her internalization of dominant ideas about what constitutes proper womanhood.

Logan Killicks is the much older man of property who becomes Janie's first husband. He is shrewd enough to acquire the attractive teenager but has no idea how to keep Janie, the romantic dreamer and natural woman. One-dimensional Logan is practical, hardworking, and has no sense of romance; his pedestrian attitude toward Janie leaves her cold, their predictable and staid relationship representing just the opposite of the possibilities she saw in the Horizon. Reading her disinterest as ingratitude, Logan's response is to attempt to make Janie work alongside him. Ambitious, pompous, and chauvinistic Joe (Jody) Starks comes down the road one day and, reminding Janie of the Horizon, eventually convinces her to leave Logan. He becomes Janie's prosperous second husband and the first mayor of Eatonville, Florida. Joe's plans for Janie are almost the opposite of Logan's: he wants to put her on a pedestal. Neither Joe nor Logan considers that Janie's desires might run counter to their plans for her life. Thus, Janie's second marriage deteriorates as Janie's voice and desire are subjugated to Joe's. Janie nevertheless grows in self-knowledge and bides her time. After some twenty years of marriage, Joe Starks dies believing that Janie has used conjure to fix him.

Tea Cake, an itinerant laborer whose real name is Vergible Woods, becomes Janie's third husband. Human and therefore flawed, Tea Cake is nevertheless in touch with his natural and organic self and thus becomes the soul mate Janie has been seeking. Rather than attempt to shape her according to his vision, Tea Cake embraces and appreciates her as she is. With Tea Cake's entrance, the pear blossom that signifies her sexual awakening returns; her relationship with Tea Cake fulfills the promise of real marriage Janie had witnessed as she lay on her back under the blossoming pear tree in her adolescence. Bitten by a rabid dog while trying to save Janie's life, he gradually loses his sanity. In madness, he tries to kill Janie, but she kills him in self-defense.

## The surface narrative

While the opening scenes of *Their Eyes Were Watching God* set Janie up as the storyteller, the narrative unfolds through a third-person point of view. The story begins with an ode to the Horizon and Janie Crawford's return to Eatonville after having buried Tea Cake and stood trial for killing him. Eatonville folk witness her return and offer generally negative speculations about what has happened to her in the months since she left Eatonville with the much younger Tea Cake. Phoeby Watson decides that she will take her friend some food, hear her story from her own mouth, and report back. Speaking from the third-person perspective, Janie begins with an abbreviated story of her youth, explaining that she was raised by her grandmother after her mother disappeared. She had grown up, literally in the backyard of the white folks who employed Nanny, playing with white children, thinking herself just like them before she recognized her difference as the dark child among others in a photograph. Realizing how important it was for Janie to know the difference, Nanny moved away from her employer's premises; she and Janie moved into their own home and Janie came of age there. Janie described her sexual awakening in the following passage:

> She [Janie] was stretched on her back beneath the pear tree soaking in the alto chant of the visiting bees, the gold of the sun and the panting breath of the breeze when the inaudible voice of it all came to her. She saw a dust-bearing bee sink into the sanctum of a bloom; the thousand sister-calyxes arch to meet the love embrace and the ecstatic shiver of the tree from root to tiniest branch creaming in every blossom and frothing with delight. So this was a marriage! She had been summoned to behold a revelation. Then Janie felt a pain remorseless sweet that left her limp and languid.[5]

Throughout Janie's story, the pear blossom becomes a recurring metaphor for awakening possibility and more specifically for Janie's sexual awakening; Janie's "pain remorseless sweet" is clearly a euphemism for orgasm, a euphemism Hurston employs later in her protagonist's response to a forced de-flowering in *Seraph on the Suwanee*. Not long after Janie's pear blossom experience, Nanny awoke from a nap just in time to see Janie kissing Johnny Taylor.

Outraged and apprehensive about Janie's future, she quickly set plans for Janie's marriage to Logan Killicks in motion. As a man of property, Killicks could provide attractive but poor Janie Crawford with the economic protection that property ownership brings while saving her from the potential social and economic catastrophe of unwed motherhood. Janie enters the marriage to Logan reluctantly, but she tries to make the most of an undesirable situation. The relationship lacked key elements of love, desire, or even sexual pleasure. When she complained to Nanny of the problems in her marriage, Janie received a stern rebuke for failing to realize how much worse her life could be. Understanding that life with Logan represented neither the Horizon (possibility) nor the sexual expression associated with life, spring, and the pear tree in bloom, Janie returned to Logan and tried to make the best of an unhappy situation. Logan believed Janie was simply ungrateful, and he balked at continuing to provide her such a soft existence; he insisted that she should start helping him with the farm work. Janie, in turn, balked at the idea of becoming what amounted to a work mule; fortunately, the opportunity to leave her first marriage presented itself before she could be transformed into a work mule when Joe Starks happened down the road one day.

Starks was immediately taken by Janie's beauty and set about acquiring her for himself. After several secret meetings Janie and Jody (her pet name for Starks) ran away together; they married and continued on to Eatonville. Though Jody did not represent the pear tree in bloom for Janie any more than Logan did, he represented the Horizon and possibility. Like Janie, he was a dreamer. In Eatonville, Joe bought land to expand the town, set up a general store, and quickly made back his initial investment; he was elected Eatonville's first mayor and became the town's most prosperous citizen. Janie's initial happiness with Jody receded when she understood that his plans for her would preclude her from expressing herself naturally in the world. Like Nanny, he wanted Janie to sit on a pedestal, to assume the status typically assigned to the wives of affluent white men. His initial romancing of her had given way to the deep-seated chauvinism at his core, the protection he offered coming in the form of almost total subjugation of her self-expression. The marriage thus stifled Janie's natural way of being in the world. Fond of the lying contests and other oral folk traditions that took place on the porch of the Starkses' general store, Janie could not join in the fun and games without risking the ire and rebuke of her husband. After Joe witnessed a townsman stealthily stroking Janie's long, black hair, he insisted that while in public she should cover her hair with a scarf. Janie abided by her husband's wishes and their economic prosperity increased while their relationship deteriorated; she simply placed an essential aspect of her evolving self-awareness on hold.

Over the years, she suffered the many slights that Joe hurled her way; then, one day when she felt he had gone too far with a comment about the lessening attractiveness of her posterior, she finally found her voice. In the ensuing public exchange, Janie beat Joe at specifying (playing the dozens) by suggesting that his manhood was certainly not what it used to be, that – undressed – he looked like the "change of life." Joe was simply nonplussed. She had bested Joe with her words. Not long after his public undressing, middle-aged Joe became ill and, as his health deteriorated, he became increasingly suspicious of Janie. He believed she had been involved in working a Hoodoo curse on him, and he died thinking her his worst enemy. His death freed thirtysomething Janie from the stifling constraints of the marriage.

One day a sexy slacker named Tea Cake appeared at the general store. Over a decade younger than Janie, Tea Cake appealed to the latent adolescent in her; he represented to Janie the pear blossom and natural sexual expression. After some initial trepidation on Janie's part, the two began an organic and passionate affair, eventually leaving Eatonville to travel south and work among common laborers in Belle Glade – literally in the muck of the Florida Everglades. Tea Cake eventually became Janie's third husband; their relationship served as the final leg of Janie's journey to self. Importantly, Hurston depicts their relationship as realistic rather than idealized. Tea Cake was not without his own chauvinistic attitudes; at one point he slapped Janie to emphasize his manliness and his masculine control in their relationship. Janie's jealous response to another scenario involving a woman named Nunkie hinted at Tea Cake's infidelity. Tea Cake was also a gambler who took money from Janie's purse without her permission and with the explanation (much later) that he wanted to turn it into more money so that he could afford to provide properly for her. That Janie devoted herself to Tea Cake and considered him the love of her life in spite of his flaws suggests that she was aware of her own flawed humanity. During a flood that followed a hurricane, a rabid dog bit Tea Cake, who subsequently developed rabies. In an advanced state of dementia, Tea Cake threatened to shoot Janie and she shot him in self-defense. Janie faced trial for killing Tea Cake; acquitted, she returned alone to Eatonville and the money and property she had left behind. The novel ends with Janie having come full circle, having appropriated the power of the Word through the recitation of her story to Phoeby. She stresses the importance of her relationship with Tea Cake, recounting many loving memories of their short time together and pronouncing him the love of her life.

## Analysis

A basic quest narrative, the central story of *Their Eyes Were Watching God* features a young woman's spiritual, emotional, and physical journey toward self-actualization. Readers are invited to experience the novel as an odyssey, as a series of adventures through which the protagonist obtains experience and, increasingly, self-knowledge. It also treats the subject of black female sexuality realistically, making it an intrinsic aspect of the protagonist's process of self-actualization. Hurston also illustrates her amazing capacity for metaphor in the many symbolic uses of trees throughout the novel to mark not only the protagonist's own desires but also the distance between her desires and the other persons in her orbit. Finally, Hurston's intimate knowledge of the oral folk vernacular peculiar to that part of Florida, and her intimate engagement with language assist in giving her work the ring of authenticity. Her incorporation of folk tales, lying contests, and other aspects of the oral tradition, adds dimension and texture to her narrative. The focus on the spoken word is particularly appropriate in a novel whose central project is giving voice to the heroine's journey toward self-knowledge.

While critics disagree as to whether Janie actually achieves voice in the narrative because the protagonist renders the story in the third person, the narrative is based on Janie's recollections as told to her friend Phoeby. Janie's desire for self-knowledge gained through experience is expressed in opening and recurrent references to 'the Horizon.' Slavery's legacy of the sexual abuse and exploitation of black women, embodied in Nanny's story, was one of the primary obstacles to Janie's autonomous self and sexual development. *Their Eyes Were Watching God* returns to this history via Janie's recollection of Nanny's experiences under slavery and Leafy's rape in freedom. In order to gain her own experience, Janie needed to distance herself from her grandmother's experience and the historical narrative that had shaped it. Janie believed she was making a major move toward the Horizon when she left Logan Killicks to become Mrs. Joe Starks. She later realized that the move only served to provide her a supporting role in her new husband's vision of the possibilities for *his* life and *his* concept of the Horizon. Nevertheless, her decidedly unhappy marriage to Joe Starks put her in the right place at the right time for Tea Cake to make his appearance. For some critics, Tea Cake functions as a trickster in the sense that it is through her relationship with him that Janie experiences a most profound transformation; her "soul crawled out from its hiding place."[6] In her statement to Phoeby before she left with Tea Cake, "Ah done lived Grandma's way, now Ah means tuh live mine,"[7] Janie expressed her understanding of freedom by articulating her awareness that she has options and by exercising one of the options available to her. Her feeling upon reaching the Everglades was that everything was big and new, an expression often associated with arrival at a place of salvation and renewal, a Promised Land, so to speak. Ultimately the relationship with Tea Cake, like the ones with Logan and Joe, served as a vehicle through which Janie gained experience and self-knowledge. The experience she obtained from liv-ing and working in the muck, from her exultant love relationship, and from the simultaneous achievement of sexual fulfillment and respectability, distanced Janie from the constraining effects of the narrative that had served to limit her grandmother's options for self-actualization.

Janie's grandmother had been subject to coerced sexual relations with the slavemaster who owned her. Janie tells Phoeby that a week after her Nanny had given birth to Leafy, her master had come for the last time to her cabin as he was about to leave for Civil War duty:

> "They was all cheerin' and cryin' and shoutin' for de men that was ridin' off. Ah couldn't see nothin' cause yo' mama wasn't but a week old, and Ah was flat uh mah back. But pretty soon he let on he forgot somethin' and run into mah cabin and *made me let down mah hair* for de last time. He sorta wropped his hand in it, pulled mah big toe, lak he always done, and was gone *after de rest* lak lightnin'. . . ."[8]    (my emphasis)

Hurston's capacity for euphemism and ambiguity is evident here. The reader must decide what it means to "let one's hair down", or to what exactly "after de rest" refers. Is the slavemaster simply saying goodbye to a favorite concubine before he goes off to fight for her continued enslavement, or is he there for one last sexual encounter before riding off to fight for her continued enslavement? Nanny's memory of her own sexual exploitation under slavery, and Janie's mother's rape following slavery, drove her desire to secure the best possible protection for her beloved granddaughter; she saw Janie's best option in the arranged marriage to Logan Killicks. Janie recalls Nanny's words:

> "Ah was born back due in slavery so it wasn't for me to fulfill my dreams of what a woman oughta be and to do. . . . Ah didn't want to be used for a work-ox and a brood-sow and Ah didn't want mah daughter used dat way neither. It sho wasn't mah will for things to happen lak they did. Ah even hated de way you was born. But, all the same Ah said thank God, Ah got another chance. Ah wanted to preach a great sermon about colored women sittin' on high, but there wasn't no pulpit for me. . . . So whilst I was tendin' you of nights Ah said I'd save de text for you."[9]

Nanny's desire to raise Janie to be a "respectable" black woman also suggests an engagement with Cult of True Womanhood ideology, a nineteenth-century ideology of womanhood that placed black women on the licentious end of a spectrum against its opposite: bourgeois white women who exhibited the qualities of domesticity, piety, purity, and submissiveness – true women. The protected bourgeois wife was placed on a pedestal that served both to protect and to constrict. Buying into the dominant ideology of true womanhood, Nanny sought to fulfill her own unfulfilled desire for the pedestal through Janie; her desire to make Janie "respectable" temporarily supplants Janie's own romantic dreams of the pear blossom when Nanny marries her off to Logan Killicks. Logan Killicks' plan to turn Janie into a farm hand, to place her behind a mule rather than on a pedestal, becomes particularly ironic.

While at least one celebrated feminist scholar has described Janie Crawford Killicks Starks Woods as a woman "in search of an orgasm,"[10] clearly, Janie's quest for knowledge through experience has more to do with her desire to expand the meaning of black female respectability – to include the full expression of her sexuality. At the time, such an insistence represented a radical turn for a black female protagonist. Hurston's choice to represent an erotic young black female character flew in the face of prescriptive advice from the black literary establishment to avoid subject matter that reinforced the dominant image of the wanton, licentious black woman. The tendency had been to draw silence around black female sexuality as a response to an automatic stigmatization of black female sexuality. While Hurston compromised by cloaking Janie's sexual desire in the pear blossom metaphor, she nevertheless broke new ground for black women writers with her insistence on making sexuality and sexual expression essential aspects of the heroine's quest and thus part of the subjectivity she asserts. She explicitly links intensely sensual scenes with her heroine's quest for fulfillment and consistently returns to the language and imagery of the scene depicting Janie's first sexual climax under the pear tree as an epiphany related to self-knowledge.

The pear tree metaphor is one of numerous tree metaphors used throughout *Their Eyes Were Watching God*. For example, Janie begins her recital to Phoeby by saying that "Janie saw her life like a great tree in leaf with the things suffered, things enjoyed, things done and undone. Dawn and doom was in the branches."[11] The metaphor symbolizes a life in full bloom, a life full of the comic and the tragic, a life full of learning experiences. The fully developed tree serves as fulfillment of the adolescent wish expressed in the following: "Oh to be a pear tree – any tree in bloom! With kissing bees singing of the beginning of the world! She was sixteen. She had glossy leaves and bursting buds and she wanted to struggle with life but it seemed to elude her. Where were the singing bees for her? Nothing on the place nor in her grandma's house answered her."[12] Janie describes Nanny's head and face (after Nanny witnesses the kiss between Johnny Taylor and Janie) as resembling "the standing roots of some old tree that had been torn away by storm."[13] Hurston's use of opposing metaphors for Janie's awakening sexual desire and Nanny's reaction to it reflects the tension between Nanny's vision rooted in slavery and its aftermath and Janie's desire to transcend the limits of Nanny's vision. Similarly, Logan Killicks represents the obverse of Janie's budding pear tree; she sees his many acres as "a stump in the middle of the woods where nobody had ever been." In touch with nature on an organic level, Janie "knew things that nobody had ever told her . . . the words of the trees and the wind." Janie and Joe Starks first talk under a tree and later meet daily "in the scrub oaks across the road." While Joe "did not represent sunup and pollen and blooming trees," he did represent the Horizon. While "flower dust and springtime" characterize Janie's initial impression of marriage to Joe, that image dissipates as his chauvinism is manifested in his increasing domination and control over her. Jody silences her, slaps her, and makes her cover her hair. The pear tree returns with Tea Cake; Janie recalls that, "He looked like the love thoughts of women. He could be a bee to a blossom – a pear tree blossom in the spring. He seemed to be crushing scent out of the world with his footsteps. Crushing aromatic herbs with every step he took. Spices hung from him. He was a glance from God."[14] Hurston's use of trees and other natural images throughout the novel help to shore up her overall depiction of Janie as a woman in touch with nature on an elemental, organic level, and for whom the desire for the sexual and other experiences that will shape her identity is as natural as the trees, flowers, and even the hurricane she experiences in the Everglades – where she undergoes the most intense aspect of her transformation.

In keeping with the organic nature of *Their Eyes Were Watching God*, Hurston relies heavily on oral forms, including folk tales, songs, proverbs, shouts, sermons, and so on; in particular, Janie tells her story in her rural southern black vernacular. *Their Eyes Were Watching God* proceeds from Janie's telling of her own story to Phoeby, and the narrative contains numerous other examples of speechmaking and storytelling which often incorporate elements of the oral tradition. The most obvious examples of the signal importance of orality and voice in the narrative are Joe Starks's speeches, the lies and tales that emerge during conversations on the porch of Starks's general store, and Janie's besting of Joe Starks during their specifying event that ends in Joe's undressing. The discussions about Matt Bonner's mule include several stories or lies and even a eulogy.[15]

Many of the tales that emerge from the general-store porch are used to characterize relationships between men and women, an issue raised in the novel's opening paragraphs. According to Daphne Lamothe, in "Vodou Imagery," the opening paragraphs of *Their Eyes Were Watching God* function much like the chant, song, or prayer that begins every Voodoo ceremony. The novel's opening also invokes Legba, "the keeper of the crossroads, which is the gateway between the spiritual and material worlds."[16] Hurston incorporates numerous additional elements of Voodoo and Hoodoo into the novel and the result is a narrative that functions much like a work of conjure, as a ritual through which Janie becomes the woman she desires to become; *Their Eyes Were Watching God* becomes its own organic oral form.

## Tell My Horse (1938)

### Time period and setting

Hurston conducted the research for *Tell My Horse* during 1936 and 1937. The folklore, ceremonies, and rituals she includes in the volume represent centuries of knowledge and practice. A variety of locations in Jamaica and Haiti are featured. In Jamaica, Hurston visits St. Mary's parish and interacts with a Pocomania cult. She travels to what she calls the best place in the parish, Port Maria, for a "curry goat feed." Next, she visits the Maroons at Accompong to experience a wild-boar hunt and a jerk barbecue; from there, she travels to the mountains of St. Thomas.

### Characters

The characters in *Tell My Horse* are the many Jamaicans and Haitians Hurston encounters in her travels and investigations. Because of her very different approaches to the two nations, and because she spent much more time in Haiti than in Jamaica, it is much easier to list some of her significant contacts in Jamaica. Her interactions with groups of Jamaicans were very similar to her interactions with groups of southerners in the United States South. She described Norman W. Manley as a "brilliant young barrister" who could rival Clarence Darrow in the courtroom. She spends time among the Pocomania cult and its leaders, Brother Levi and Mother Saul. Hurston describes Mother Saul as "the most regal woman since Sheba went to see Solomon."[17] Witnessing the cult's open air "Sun Dial" ceremony, she takes note of the roles, or "characters," assumed by various rite participants: The Shepherd, the Sword Boy, the Symbol Boy, the Unter Boy, the Governess, and the Shepherd Boy. Affluent bachelor and plantation owner C. I. Magnus hosts a "curry goat feed" at Port Maria. The meal (part of a pre-wedding celebration) is prepared by "Hindoos" and guests include Dr. Leslie, Claude Bell (Superintendent of Public Works for

St. Mary's), Rupert and O. S. Meikle (brothers who came in first and second in the storytelling contest), Larry Coke, J. T. Robertson, Reginald Beckford, some "very pretty half-Chinese girls," and others.

At the Accompong Maroon settlement, Hurston encounters Colonel Rowe and his extended family, which includes his offspring and grandchildren; one motherless child in particular touches her heart – little Tom, the much abused and ill-treated child of one of the Colonel's sons. Because the boy's father has proven to be disloyal, lazy, and shiftless, the little boy is judged to be fruit of a bad seed and thus doomed to turn out just like his father. Much of Hurston's time is spent in the company of Rowe and the chief medicine man for Accompong, to whom she refers as Medicine Man. Hurston persuades some of the men at Accompong to stage a wild-boar hunt, and she joins the hunting party which includes Rowe, his brother Esau, Tom Colly, Colly's sons and son-in-law, and the son-in-law's son. At St. Thomas – where Joe Forsythe serves as her traveling companion – Hurston spends time learning about ceremonies for the dead and the family members left behind. Old district nurses called Nanas play essential roles in the ceremonies, which involve numerous other participants in a variety of roles, but few of them are mentioned by name. One exception is Zachariah, "the Power," an exceptional dancer who dominates during the most climactic part of a ritual ceremony.

## Format and contents

Hurston dedicates *Tell My Horse* to Carl Van Vechten, whom she first met in 1925 at an *Opportunity* magazine awards dinner. "Tell my horse," or *parlay cheval ou* in Creole, is a phrase Hurston heard often during her time in Haiti. According to lore, they are words uttered by Guede (pronounced "geeday"), a Voodoo god/loa/deity characterized as powerful and boisterous. Guede makes himself known by mounting or possessing someone and speaking through him or her. According to Hurston, peasants in Haiti used the phrase as a disclaimer, invoking Guede as the force behind their caustic or frank comments. Thus, the phrase and the loa are identified with the common folk who do not bite their tongues or pull punches. The title is an apt one for a volume in which Hurston speaks so frankly about race, class, politics, and (particularly) gender relations in Jamaica and Haiti. As critics have correctly noted, the volume unfolds as a too hastily written montage of folklore, political reporting and commentary, and even travelogue. In his Foreword to a 1990 edition of the novel, author Ishmael Reed notes that the volume's disjointed (though chronological) structure and sometimes contradictory narrative are best appreciated when viewed through the lens of postmodernism.

Hurston divided the collection into three parts. Part one follows her experiences in Jamaica, is aptly titled "Jamaica," and contains five chapters: "The Rooster's Nest," "Curry Goat," "Hunting the Wild Hog," "Night Song after Death," and "Women in the Caribbean." Parts two and three detail her experiences in Haiti and are titled "Politics and Personalities of Haiti" and "Voodoo in Haiti," respectively. Part two contains four chapters: "Rebirth of a Nation," "The Next Hundred Years," "The Black Joan of Arc," and "Death of Leconte." Part three is comprised of nine chapters: "Voodoo and Voodoo Gods," "Isle de la Gonave," "Archahaie and What It Means," "Zombies," "Secte Rouge," "Parlay Cheval Ou," "Graveyard Dirt and Other Poisons," "Doctor Reser," and "God and the Pintards." An appendix is divided into two parts, "Songs of Worship to Voodoo Gods," and "Miscellaneous Songs."

Hurston's presence as narrator/observer/participant/researcher is again apparent as it was during her time in the American South collecting material for *Mules and Men*. While the volume is less coherent than *Mules and Men* – because it lacks the sustained narrative and thus cohesiveness of the former volume – once again Hurston's immersion in the culture under study results in a rich and multi-dimensional collection unlike anything that had been produced before. She did not write a formal introduction for the volume, opting instead to begin with chapter one whose title, "The Rooster's Nest," signifies Hurston's impression of Jamaican society as undervaluing its female members.

The chapter begins benignly enough with a salute to the value of Jamaica as a resource for natural medicines. Next, the narrator focuses on the Pocomania cult and describes in some detail their "Sun Dial" ceremony, so named because it lasts for twenty-four hours. The chapter segues to a discussion of caste, color, and social stratification on the island, with Hurston concluding that, typical of colonized people, everyone aspires to be as British as possible. Gradually, the meaning of the chapter's title becomes clear; it refers to the situation produced by liaisons between black Jamaican women and Englishmen or Scotsmen. The resulting "pink" offspring is very proud of the fact of her or his father; however, the relationship to the black mother is ignored or hidden. The effect is that the "pink" offspring seems to have no mother (the hen), only a father (the rooster). She expresses her disdain for "pink Jamaicans" through ridicule and ends the short chapter with the hope that darker-skinned Jamaicans continue to grow in self-respect and that their intrinsic worth and tangible contributions to Jamaican culture will be recognized. Ultimately, the chapter provides a commentary on color caste prejudice in Jamaica and reflects Hurston's pride in her African heritage.

Chapter 2, "Curry Goat," is set at St. Mary's Port. Hurston details the festivities surrounding a "curry goat feed," which includes the preliminary storytelling contests, songs, and poking fun at one another over cock soup. The preliminaries are followed by ram goat and rice, which is topped off with banana dumplings dipped in *suruwa* sauce. Everything is washed down with rum which makes for a highly festive mood as prizes are given for best storyteller and the band cranks out the music for dancing. The meal is part of the preparation for a wedding that takes place the following day. After a particularly animated exchange about women's subordination in Jamaican society with a decidedly chauvinist young Jamaican man who articulates his very narrow concept of gender, Hurston persuades him to help her gain access to information about the preparation process young girls undergo for marriage or to become the mistresses of affluent men. The process, she learns, is presided over by specialists, old women, who spend days teaching the young virgin how to become simultaneously innocent and competent. The girl is taught how to position herself on her first night with the man; she must be on the floor with only the soles of her feet and her shoulders touching it. The specialist teaches her how to control her inner and outer body muscles in order to enhance his pleasure. The final process of preparation begins with a "balm bath" to rid the girl of inhibitions. This herbal bath is followed by a full body herb and oil massage, after which the breasts are bathed several times in special water and then massaged using a special fingertip motion that is then carried across the entire body. During this process, the girl receives a sip of ganga-steeped rum whenever she swoons, for by the time she reaches this phase of the preparation process she is in a "twilight state of awareness."[18] Such detail as Hurston provides in her matter-of-fact descriptions of the varying rituals, ceremonies, and practices allows the reader to judge for herself whether the culture is inherently misogynist. That she describes no similar process for preparing a man for his first night with his bride or new mistress is very telling. The subtle critique of gender relations that Hurston made in *Mules and Men* by moving from the rigidly gendered space of Eatonville, to her descriptions of the somewhat androgynous Big Sweet, and finally to the New Orleans area where – within the realm of Hoodoo – gender was more balanced is here much more explicit; it becomes increasingly so as the Jamaica section proceeds.

In chapter 3, Hurston recalls a visit with the self-governing Maroons of Accompong. There she discovered a remarkable medicine man that people came from miles around to see. Clearly a source for Hurston's Moses in *Moses, Man of the Mountain*, Medicine Man's conjure powers include the ability to make frogs on a nearby mountain stop chirping in a flash; he teaches Hurston about the medicinal benefits of roots and herbs as well as the harmful benefits of certain plants. As the title "Hunting the Wild Hog" suggests however, much of the chapter is devoted to an account of Hurston's experience camping out with Maroons on a hunting expedition during which they catch, cook, and eat wild boar. Again, Hurston reveals the process in vivid, colorful, and exciting language, right down to the manner in which the boar is captured, prepared, cooked overnight in jerk spices, and consumed the next morning.

Chapter 4, "Night Song after Death," recounts an elaborate ritual performed following death to prevent the duppy – the deceased *sans* heart and mind – from leaving the grave and returning to do harm to the living. People believe the duppy is capable of the evil that resides in humans but which is controlled so long as the person has a functioning heart and brain. Hurston explains how Nanas prepare the deceased's body, washing it, drying it, and then rubbing lime and nutmeg under its arms and between its legs. The body is then placed in a coffin with a pillow containing parched peas, corn, and coffee beans. Next, nails are driven through the shirt cuffs and the sock heels into the coffin in an attempt to keep the duppy from leaving the grave. The subsequent grave digging and interment involve much consumption of rum and, for nine nights following the burial, family and friends gather for something resembling wakes. The nine nights, during which ceremonies involving singing, dancing, drinking, and eating occur, are meant to force the duppy to stay in its grave so that it has no chance to do evil.

The final chapter of part one, "Women in the Caribbean," contains Hurston's further indictment of what she described as misogynist Caribbean (particularly Jamaican) culture. To make her case, she relates several stories about women's abuse and exploitation. In one, a pretty brown skin girl feels fortunate when a Mulatto man shows interest in her. The man courts her for several months and finally forces himself on her before admitting that he is scheduled to marry someone else the following day. That reminder of her lower caste status not being sufficient, years later he learns that she is to be married and halts the process by telling her intended groom that the woman is not a virgin. In a further illustration of the inferior status of women in Haitian society, Hurston explains that Haitian law does not allow a woman to accuse a man who is not her husband of being the father of her child. Thus, men who manage to father children out of wedlock bear no legal obligation to the child or its mother. To get a woman into bed, Hurston reports, some men go as far as marrying her and then claiming that she was not a virgin on the wedding night. The bride cannot then claim virginity because the marriage has to be consummated in order for the husband to make the charge. The inclusion of such stories reveals Hurston's strong pro-woman consciousness, though her harsh critique of women's status in Jamaica reflects a bit of selective blindness in her assertions about the comparatively privileged status of women in the United States at the time.

Part two turns to Haiti's social and political climate. Hurston's title for chapter 6, "Rebirth of a Nation," no doubt signifies on the hugely popular 1915 D. W. Griffith film focusing on the birth of the Ku Klux Klan. The chapter provides a summary of the late eighteenth-century Haitian revolution, with profiles of the revolution's leaders (Toussaint L'Ouverture, Christophe, Pétion, and Dessalines) and assessments of the obstacles they faced not only in driving out the French but also in leading a colony of formerly enslaved persons toward self-government. Hurston's assessments of the attitudes of newly freed persons parallel to some extent that of the newly freed Hebrews in *Moses, Man of the Mountain.* In the next chapter, she offers a somewhat arbitrary account of Haitian affairs and internal politics that shaped Haitian identity, this time for the over one hundred years following the revolution until the time of her visit. In both chapters, as she had done in the section on Jamaica, Hurston notes caste and color divisions and prejudices. Both chapters are obviously heavily influenced by Hurston's own subjectivity; even more problematic than her attempt at a historical narrative of Haiti is her apparent desire to sum up its national character.

In this attempt, she sometimes resorted to overgeneralizations and stereotypes such as when she writes the following after discussing the disillusionment that leaders of the Haitian revolution experienced:

> Perhaps it was in this way that Haitians began to deceive themselves about actualities and to throw a gloss over facts. Certainly at the present time the art of saying what one would like to be believed instead of the glaring fact is highly developed in Haiti. And when an unpleasant truth must be acknowledged a childish and fantastic explanation is ready at hand. More often it is an explanation that nobody but an idiot could accept but it is told to intelligent people with an air of gravity. This lying habit goes from the thatched hut to the mansion, the only differences being in the things that are lied about. The upper class lie about the things for the most part that touch their pride. The peasant lies about things that affect his well-being like work, and food, and small change.[19]

In effect, she proclaims all Haitians to be avid liars, though she could not possibly have interacted with enough Haitians during her time there to make such a judgment.

Hurston continues to reveal Haiti's unique and – for many – long hidden history in chapter 8 with the story of the woman called the black Joan of

Arc, Celestina Simon. Simon was a Voodoo priestess and daughter of General François Antoine Simon who served as Haiti's president in the south from 1908 until 1911. The chapter charts the father's reign and ultimate overthrow, followed by his voluntary exile to Jamaica. In retelling the story of Celestina and her father, Hurston calls attention to the profound role that Voodoo played in both their lives – particularly its role in initially bringing General Simon to power. In the next chapter, Hurston focuses on the death of Cincinnatus Leconte, the Haitian leader responsible for driving Simon from office. Her goal, she explains, is to correct the historical record (which says that Leconte died when his palace was destroyed by an explosion) by including the people's account of his actual death by assassination. Through a series of conversations, she reconstructs the likely scenario for Leconte's assassination – the palace explosion being a means of covering up the fact that he had already been murdered through a conspiracy set in motion by members of his own regime. She also praises the American occupation of Haiti between 1915 and 1934.

In part three of *Tell My Horse*, Hurston focuses specifically on Voodoo in Haiti. As she had done in her work on Hoodoo in the southern United States, she locates the origins of Voodoo "in the beginning" when the universe came into being through a major act of conjure. She explains that Voodoo is centered on creation and life; natural forces such as the sun and water serve as the foci of its worship. She represents it as a religion, inscribed with both male and female attributes and older than Christianity, Islam, and Buddhism. As with the section on Jamaica, Hurston invokes the beauty of the landscape and sacred zones, giving the volume an aura of travelogue as a backdrop to her cataloguing and descriptions of Voodoo's major loas/gods/deities. We learn, for example, that the Rada group of deities is considered "good," while the Petro group is considered "bad." Hurston also devotes a good deal of space to information about mortals being mounted or taken over by dangerous Petro gods. When Hurston returned to Haiti to focus specifically on the Petro gods, she was stricken with a severe stomach ailment that ultimately compelled her to leave Haiti and return to the States.

Despite having been sworn to secrecy, Hurston uses part three to recount her experiences deep in the heart of the Haitian bush. Indeed, the suggestion is that her severe illness was punishment for her lack of secrecy, including the photographing of zombie Felicia Felix-Mentor in Gonaives. A zombie is a shell of a human being; the mind is effectively decimated while the body remains intact. While doctors speculate that the condition is caused by the administering of a mind-decimating poisonous weed, Hurston ascribes the evil of zombie-making to *bocors* and explains that it is impossible to acquire the list of ingredients that would produce a zombie. The volume contains numerous other photos depicting important figures, landmarks, dances and a variety of activities. The result is a representation of Vodun as a legitimate religion. Hurston's treatment is more respectable and less sensationalized than the way in which Vodun had traditionally been represented to American audiences. *Tell My Horse* was later published in Great Britain as *Voodoo Gods: An Inquiry into Native Myths and Magic in Jamaica and Haiti* (1939).

## Moses, Man of the Mountain (1939)

### Time period and setting

Hurston uses the mythic story of Moses, best recognized in western culture as the biblical Hebrew hero of the book of Exodus who led his people out of Egyptian bondage into Canaan/Israel/the Promised Land, to create an allegory of African American life from slavery to freedom. Thus, the time period reflects that of the biblical Exodus and also the centuries of American slavery and race-based discrimination that began in the New World in the seventeenth century. While the basic Moses story is common to a number of different cultures and ethnic groups, Hurston uses traditional biblical settings for her story: Egypt, Goshen (the slave ghetto), the Red Sea, Midian, Koptos, and the wilderness of newfound freedom on the way to the Promised Land. Because Hurston is more interested in the Moses story as an example of individual self-determination and leadership, she is less attentive to landscape detail here than in her other novels, where place (particularly specific areas of her native Florida) plays such an important role. Her story is presented as timeless, one that is relevant for any group or individual that desires to experience the full meaning of freedom.

### Major characters

Moses is raised as an Egyptian prince, though he is rumored to be the son of enslaved Hebrews, Jochebed and Amram. Like the Hebrew mother in the Bible story, Jochebed places her infant son in a basket on the river to protect him from Pharoah's police and then gives her daughter Miriam the responsibility of watching the infant. Miriam falls asleep and when she awakens, she has lost sight of her brother. She makes up a story that Pharoah's daughter took the child and adopted him as her own. Hurston slants the ambiguity surrounding Moses' ethnic origin toward his being the Egyptian son of the Princess, rather than Hebrew. Moses' unique character is revealed through his interactions with others. For example, he finds an early mentor in Mentu, a minor conjurer who serves as stableman for the royal family. An apt student, Moses respects Mentu and gains knowledge and wisdom from him, including military strategy, how to communicate with animals, and how to ride a horse. Under his tutelage, Moses becomes the mightiest soldier in the land and a purveyor of organic folk wisdom. Like the biblical Moses, he is a natural born leader, a man of integrity and compassion who shuns the external accoutrements and adornments that typically accompany his position. Most significantly, Mentu teaches Moses about the *Book of Thoth*. Moses goes into exile after killing one of Pharoah's overseers who is brutally assaulting a Hebrew slave. He again proves an apt student under the tutelage of an even greater teacher, who eventually convinces him to accept the call to lead the enslaved Hebrews (who actually speak an African American dialect) out of Egypt and convince them to follow the one true God. Pharoah Ta-Phar is Moses' uncle, antithesis, and chief antagonist; he is both jealous of Moses and also the kind of selfish, proud, and vain leader Moses could never be; Ta-Phar welcomes the external trappings that come with position. Under his rule, the Hebrews experience a harsher form of slavery than they experienced under his father.

Miriam is the daughter of Jochebed and Amram who falls asleep and then lies about what happened to her infant brother. As an adult and during the Exodus out of Egypt, Miriam becomes a prophetess and leader among Hebrew women. Vain and hungry for power, she earns the ire of Moses and he turns her into a leper. Miriam's brother Aaron also becomes a leader among the Hebrews. Like Miriam, he craves power, riches, and respect; like Miriam he is also jealous of Moses' power and the respect he receives. Aaron works directly in contravention to Moses' teachings about the one true God when he constructs a golden calf as an idol and bids the Hebrews worship it. Moses knows that Aaron is, like Miriam, not good for the newly freed Hebrews. He saves them from the potential of Aaron's harmful leadership by walking him up Mt. Horeb into a death trap.

When Moses goes into exile, he meets Jethro/Ruel at Midian. Jethro is a wise prince and priest, a conjure man extraordinaire; he becomes Moses' new mentor, and his teachings complement those of Mentu. He convinces Moses to lead the Hebrews out of Egypt and toward the concept of one God. Zipporah, Jethro's very beautiful daughter, becomes Moses' second wife. (As a member of the royal family in Egypt, he had endured a troublesome relationship with his haughty, bigoted, and beautiful trophy-wife, a woman highly disdainful of rumors that he was actually Hebrew.) Zipporah's major flaw – and the sore spot for their marriage – is that she wants her husband to revel in his greatness, to accept the title of King and all its accoutrements so that she can enjoy a heightened status as well. Joshua becomes Moses' Hebrew protégé and confidant just as Moses had been the protégé and confidant of Jethro and (to a lesser extent) Mentu. Moses teaches Joshua reading, writing, military strategy, and helps him access natural wisdoms. Moses sees in Joshua the qualities of leadership that the Hebrews will need as they make the transition from slavery to freedom, and thus he chooses Joshua as his successor to lead the Hebrews into the Promised Land when the time is right.

## The surface story

The germ for Hurston's treatment of the Moses story came from her 1934 short story, "The Fire and the Cloud," which is based on Deuteronomy 31–4. In "The Fire and the Cloud," Moses sits on a rock at Mt. Nebo after having led the Hebrews out of bondage and after having kept them in the wilderness for two generations. Feeling that they are not yet ready to be successful in the Promised Land, Moses muses that he wants to keep them in the wilderness a bit longer; he is prepared to die knowing that they will spend at least thirty days mourning his passing before finally crossing over into Canaan.

*Moses, Man of the Mountain* begins with a short chapter in the voice of the omniscient narrator, which tells of Pharoah's increasingly harsh decrees, the most recent being that no more male Hebrew children be born; the pronouncement sets the stage for ensuing events. Jochebed, the wife of Amram, and mother of Miriam and Aaron is about to give birth. When the child is born male, they must hide him lest the Egyptian police find him and kill him during one of their frequent and unannounced sweeps. During one sweep, Amram proposes that they kill the child to prevent the Egyptians from taking his life, but Jochebed has a better idea. She places the child in a waterproof basket on the river in the hope that an Egyptian will find the child and raise him. Young Miriam is given the responsibility of watching the basket, but she falls asleep and when she awakens the basket is no longer in sight; rather than admit that she does not know what happened to the basket, she tells her mother that she saw the Pharoah's daughter retrieve it and carry it into the Palace. Hurston thus grounds her story in the basic plot of the biblical story, but she takes creative license with certain details. In fact, Hurston's story is ambiguous as to what happened to Jochebed and Amram's son and thus also ambiguous as to Moses' true identity. The suggestion is, as noted above, that Moses is more likely the Princess's biological child and therefore African. Contrary to the biblical story, Jochebed is not taken in as a wet nurse for the child; when she applies for the position, she is told that they have no need of a wet nurse – a further suggestion that Jochebed and Amram's son did not end up in the palace.

Nevertheless, the Hebrews like the idea of a Hebrew being raised within the palace gates, and the legend of Moses develops over the years. Meanwhile, the young man grows up as royalty. He receives a high-quality formal education from Egypt's high priests and, from Mentu, he learns the art of warfare; he also acquires folk wisdom and insight into natural phenomena from Mentu. He becomes a respected and accomplished military leader and is duly rewarded with a beautiful (but somewhat shallow and haughty) wife. When she hears the rumor of Moses' possible Hebrew origins, she looks upon him with disgust; her actions delight Moses' maternal uncle Ta-Phar, who is jealous of Moses' innate superiority and military might.

While Moses always denies being Hebrew, suspicions nevertheless develop. The situation comes to a head after Moses kills an overseer who was brutally beating a slave. Moses flees into exile, crossing the Red Sea (in a scene reminiscent of John Buddy Pearson's crossing the Big Creek in *Jonah's Gourd Vine*) and traveling to Midian. At Midian he encounters Midianite leader Jethro and his family. Jethro becomes his mentor and, as Mentu had been, a surrogate father to Moses. Moses falls in love with Jethro's daughter Zipporah and they marry. He lives with the Midianites for twenty-five years. Under Jethro's tutelage, Moses learns how to speak the people's idiom, which he needs in order to communicate with them as their leader. Another aspect of his preparation for leadership involves traveling to Koptos to acquire wisdom from the *Book of Thoth*. He endures a battle with a deathless serpent in order to gain access to the sacred text, and from the text he acquires the wisdom that will allow him to "command the heavens and the earth, the abyss and the mountain, and the sea. He knew the language of the birds of the air, the creatures that people the deep and what the beasts of the wilds all said. He saw the sun and the moon and the stars of the sky as no man had ever seen them before, for a divine power was with him."[20] Still, he is not persuaded to take on the task of leading the Hebrews out of Egypt until after he witnesses a manifestation of God as a burning bush. He returns to Egypt to persuade the new Pharoah Ta-Phar to free the Hebrews.

In his various petitions before Ta-Phar, Moses draws upon the knowledge of magic he acquired from Jethro, the natural wisdom he acquired from Mentu and the *Book of Thoth*. In addition to convincing Pharoah to let the Hebrews go, Moses must also convince the Hebrews that freedom is worth seeking. After so many generations of slavery, the Hebrews have developed slave mentalities and are almost totally dependent on their masters. Not only are they suspicious of Moses but they are also not ready to embrace his concept of one God. Nevertheless, with the help of Joshua, Miriam, and Aaron, Moses succeeds in convincing the Hebrews that they should leave Egypt.

They escape through a section of the Red Sea that he knows is very shallow at a certain time, and Pharoah's pursuing army is drowned when the sea changes. Moses soon realizes, however, that the first generations of Hebrews are not ready to take on the mantle of freedom. They are also not ready to accept the idea of one God. Just as in the biblical story, Moses keeps them wandering in the wilderness for several decades. He wants the generations closest to slavery to have a chance to die off. In the meantime, Moses has groomed Joshua as his replacement, and he sends him to lead the Hebrews' into the Promised Land after they have mourned Moses's death. Looking forward to his own freedom in death, Moses climbs Mt. Nebo and, after beholding the beginning of the new nation of free people, builds himself a tomb and engages in a conversation with a wise lizard before descending the other side of the mountain. The story ends on that note.

## Analysis

Hurston published *Moses, Man of the Mountain* shortly after she had completed her research for and published *Tell My Horse*. Versions of the Moses story proliferate in the southern United States and the Caribbean. The ethical system Hurston offers through the Moses story is mediated by a number of devices (including humor, dialect, and varying modes of signifying) that are part of an African American folk aesthetic. In addition to displaying her substantial knowledge of Hoodoo and Voodoo, Hurston drew upon the basic Moses story to write an allegory for the political situation of African Americans from slavery through the 1930s and to comment on the increasingly brutal Nazi regime operating in Europe at the time.

Hurston combines her respect for Voodoo as a system of beliefs, her belief in the power of conjure, and her other view of the human being in dynamic inter-action with the natural world as a way of obtaining self-knowledge into one all-encompassing story. She depicts Moses as an extraordinary master of con-jure, a Hoodoo doctor extraordinaire, his feats second only to the male/female collaboration that gave birth to the universe. In her introduction to the novel, Hurston discusses the variety of conceptions of Moses in the world, noting that legends about Moses are sown throughout Asia, the Near East, and Africa. Thus, her agenda here is to return the story to its oral roots. For Hurston, Moses was associated with one of the Rada (*good*) gods of Haitian Vodun, Damballah. Both Moses and Damballah are associated with the serpent. While the Moses Hurston constructs in her novel is an awe-inspiring conjurer, he is not perfect. He is, however, the kind of leader Hurston feels black America sorely needs in the fourth decade of the twentieth century as the world watches events unfold in Eastern Europe.

*Moses, Man of the Mountain* also displays Hurston's most overt assessment of the political situation of black Americans from slavery through the first decades of the twentieth century. As allegory, the novel takes aim at what Hurston saw as the inadequacies of black leadership and the slave mentality that continued to plague black America at the time. Hurston felt that black people were caught up appealing to white America for approval and acceptance of them as fully human. Reading Hurston's essay, "My People, My People," alongside *Moses, Man of the Mountain* helps to amplify the philosophy she espouses in the novel. In depicting the Hebrews as not yet ready for freedom, she was pointing to African America's collective lack of psychological development beyond slavery. Hurston was well aware of racial discrimination but she also felt that all too often people used the fact of discrimination as an excuse not to do better. Thus, her treatment of the Moses story echoes her philosophical and political stance on the race question. Clearly prefiguring the meditations on freedom offered in the philosophical fictions of Charles Johnson, *Moses, Man of the Mountain* advances the idea that freedom begins in the Mind; true freedom, Hurston suggested through her plot and characterization, lay in heightened awareness, understanding, and self-determination. The novel poked fun at would-be leaders represented by the posturings of Miriam and Aaron, while offering Moses' example of selfless leadership as a model. Hurston's disenchantment with what she saw as a vacuum in black American leadership (and we must recall that one of the major black leaders at the time was Hurston's nemesis, W. E. B. Du Bois) is highly apparent in her treatment here.

*Moses, Man of the Mountain* includes themes of brutal oppression, tyrannical legal practice, and rigid segregationist policies that mirror the anti-Semitic climate of Nazi Germany. Hurston opens her novel with the issuance of Pharoah's latest in a series of anti-Hebrew edicts whose parallel in Nazi Germany existed in the series of anti-Semitic laws enacted starting in the early 1930s. Ta-Phar (and those who carried out his policies) obviously serves as a parallel to Adolf Hitler and his Nazi regime, which came to power when Hitler became Chancellor of Germany in January of 1933. Enslaved Hebrews forced to produce materials and riches for their oppressors in *Moses, Man of the Mountain* not only parallel the forced-labor system that existed under slavery but also that of Hitler's Germany. Hitler's first concentration camps appeared in 1933, not long after he came to power; as early as 1934, camp prisoners were used as forced laborers in the service of SS construction projects, and such use expanded and diversified in the ensuing decade. Testimonies of survivors tell stories of prisoners literally being worked to death in the service of Hitler's vision, just as Hurston's Hebrews are worked to death under Pharoah's increasingly harsh regime in *Moses, Man of the Mountain.*

From her first published story, through her first and second novels, Hurston drew upon her knowledge of Hoodoo and Voodoo to add flavor and texture to her characters, plots, and themes. In "John Redding Goes to Sea," a woman is suspected of sprinkling the travel dust that is responsible for John's wanderlust. In *Jonah's Gourd Vine*, Hattie Tyson uses conjure to get rid of Lucy so that she can marry John Pearson, and she continues to use conjure to keep him. In *Their Eyes Were Watching God*, Hurston models Janie on the natural way of being that is inherent to Vodun, having written the novel while she was conducting research in Haiti, and even fashions her protagonist after two Voodoo deities.[21] *Moses, Man of the Mountain* represents Hurston's most overt and extended display of her knowledge of Hoodoo and Voodoo.

## *Dust Tracks on a Road* (1942)

### Time period and setting

Hurston is elusive and evasive about the exact date of her birth; however, we know that she was born in 1891. Thus, her self-portrait covers the period from the late nineteenth century through 1941. The setting takes us from Notasulga, Alabama, to various Florida locations, New York City and its environs, various other United States locations, and several Caribbean islands.

### Major characters

The central character in any autobiography is, of course, the author. The supporting players in Hurston's life story are too numerous to list here; however, major players will be revealed in the next section. Readers may also consult Chapter 1 of this volume for biographical information on Hurston, which includes information about her family, husbands, friends, and professional associates.

### The surface story

Hurston begins her autobiography with a lie – that she was born in the "pure Negro town" of Eatonville, Florida. We know that she was born in Notasulga, Alabama, and any assertion of purity is always subject to debate. Later in the work she admits that upon arriving in Baltimore, Maryland she deliberately lied about her age in order to qualify for free public education. She is deliberately vague about her age in *Dust Tracks on a Road*, and the careful reader will notice where this happens. Still, because Hurston's family moved to Eatonville when she was very young, Eatonville is the likely geographical context for her earliest memories. She titles the first chapter "My Birthplace" and then moves quickly away from the subject of her birth to begin a long, detailed discussion of the history of Eatonville – beginning right after the Civil War with the story of three former white Union officers onboard a ship near the Brazilian coast. The chapter concludes with information about Eatonville's official incorporation on August 18,1886.

Hurston is still not ready to emerge from the shadows of her own narrative in chapter 2, which is titled "My Folks"; instead, as the title implies, she provides information about how and when her parents – John Hurston and Lucy Ann Potts – met, their courtship, and the family's move to Eatonville where they were generally prosperous. Hurston paints a picture of an almost idyllic existence with plenty of fruits from the abundant fruit trees, plenty of meat, a two-story home with ample space for the growing family, and all this surrounded by a landscape of beautiful wildflowers. She provides an overview of family life, how the household was run, and the kinds of values that were instilled in her and her seven siblings. John Hurston emerges as a man who was chauvinist and philandering as well as hardworking and talented; he provided well for his family while Lucy was alive. Hurston depicts her mother as strong-willed, rock solid, and always loyal to her unfaithful husband. Lucy Potts Hurston held hearth and home together and encouraged her children to be ambitious – to "jump at the sun." A former teacher, she felt education was the key to her children's success. Hurston concludes that despite the difficulties in her parents' relationship, they must have truly been in love. Perhaps to illustrate that marital relationships are never ideal, Hurston includes in this serious chapter about her parents an amusing story about another philandering husband and his wife's responses thereto.

In chapter 3, Hurston finally provides details about her own birth at the hands of a white male neighbor. Her mother went into labor during hog-killing time, when everyone was away; John Hurston was away preaching. According to Hurston, the white man "of many acres and things . . . knew the family well. Knowing that Papa was not at home, and that consequently there would be no fresh meat in our house, he decided to drive the five miles and bring a half of a shoat, sweet potatoes, and other garden stuff along."[22] When the man arrived, Zora had already made her way out of her mother's womb and through the birth canal onto the bed. The white man cut the umbilical cord and stayed with mother and child until the midwife arrived an hour later. The unnamed white man, Hurston tells us, came back the next day and infrequently during Hurston's youth. The chapter ends with an amusing story of how Hurston first made herself walk when a sow invaded their home intent on securing the hunk of cornbread the plump 1-year-old was eating. The chapter ends with a foreshadowing of Hurston's own desire for traveling, her wanderlust that seemed to mirror that of her father's.

The information Hurston provides in chapter 4, "The Inside Search," suggests that she was anything but a demure little girl. She was, in fact, a dedicated tomboy who destroyed her dolls and could handle her own with the rough-and-tumble neighborhood boys; she often played too rough for her female playmates. Hurston is introspective in chapter 4, recalling a time during her youth when she believed the moon followed her and only her. A naturally inquisitive child, she asked questions about everything, always probing deeper and deeper regardless of whether the answers made her happy or sad. Her greatest desire was to walk out to the Horizon from her house, which she believed was the center of the world. She dreamed of riding a fine horse "off to look at the belly-band of the world," and when her father asked the children what they wanted for Christmas that year, Zora responded that she wanted "a fine black riding horse with white leather saddle and bridles," to which her father responded with outrage and chastisement.[23] She received a doll for Christmas and decided to create her own horse in her imagination.

Chapter 4 also provides an update on the white man who assisted in her birth and who subsequently took her fishing and dispensed advice to her about how to get along in the world. His nickname for her was Snidlits because he didn't care for the name Zora. Over and over, according to Hurston, he told her "don't be a nigger," because "Niggers lie and lie!"[24] Hurston offered a weak excuse for the man, explaining that she knew his use of the term "nigger" did not include a specific racial designation. The chapter also contains another intervention from whites when two northern women visit the school and Zora shines when called upon to read. Her reward is the request for a repeat performance the following day after which she receives a cylinder containing 100 pennies. A day later, she received a further reward of three books: an Episcopal hymn book, *The Swiss Family Robinson*, and a collection of fairy tales. Still later, the northern women sent Zora a box of used clothing and more books, including *Gulliver's Travels* and *Grimm's Fairy Tales*; Zora was most impressed with a volume titled *Norse Tales*. An avid reader, she devoured these and other works. The chapter also contains information about prescient visions (or scenes) that Zora first experienced around the age of 7 and which returned at irregular intervals thereafter for some time. Interestingly, she experienced the 12 scenes after eating what she describes as a big raisin she found on a neighbor's porch.

She tells us that time would "prove the truth of her visions, for one by one they came to pass."[25] The chapter ends with Zora's expression of a "cosmic loneliness"; she feels that her childhood ended once she had experienced the visions.

Chapter 5, "Figure and Fancy," begins with Zora's thoughts on God and nature, setting up her dismissal of two churches as the most important influences in Eatonville in favor of Joe Clarke's store. Hurston treats readers to a close-up examination of how the store functions for the community, how it serves as a space where the most intimate details of the townspeople's lives are exposed and revealed. It is also the space where storytelling takes place, and Hurston credits it as a place where her own penchant for storytelling was nurtured. Her proximity to Joe Clarke's store and the storytelling that goes on there is represented as the springwell for her own development as an entertainer, storyteller, and performer. She introduces us to the Spool People she created from her mother's sewing materials, for whom she fashions stories. This is the advent of Hurston, the storyteller.

In chapter 6, Hurston recounts her mother's illness and death. Here, the work takes on a morose tone as Hurston recalls unsettling family matters that include a reminder that the Potts family never approved of Lucy's marriage "beneath her class" and another about the killing of Lucy's favorite nephew, Jimmie. Death thus takes center stage in the chapter as Hurston recalls her mother's dying requests going unfulfilled, the village turning out to mourn Lucy's passing, and the abrupt changes in the household following her mother's burial. The day after their mother was buried, siblings Bob and Sarah returned to school in Jacksonville; Zora joined them two weeks later. It was in Jacksonville that she realized her difference, that her colored-ness meant she was not standard, not the norm. She perceived that the white people in Jacksonville were different than those she had grown up around near Eatonville. Zora's natural exuberance and lack of reverence for authority got her into trouble, but she tells us that "on the whole, things went along all right." On the drive to catch her train to Jacksonville, Hurston recalls realizing the first of the twelve visions that had come to her years earlier: she was leaving home "bowed down with grief that was more than common."[26] She ends the chapter by recalling a moment when she felt sure she had seen her mother, but the woman had slipped out of sight before Zora could approach her.

Chapter 7 recalls Zora's sister's return to Eatonville two months after Zora's arrival at Jacksonville. Here, Hurston reiterates the fact that Sarah had always been the favored daughter, the one who received every indulgence and the gentlest treatment from their father. She recalls learning from Sarah of her father's new marriage, that the new wife had been outraged by Sarah's observation that the marriage had happened so soon after Lucy's death. Sarah is sent packing and, according to Hurston, new wife Mattie insists that she first be beaten (the only time her father had ever struck her) and then driven out of town. Defeated, the diminutive Sarah marries quickly (and apparently badly) and takes younger brother Everett to live with her. Hurston provides additional details about the pampered existence Sarah had enjoyed from the time she was born until her stepmother's appearance. In telling Sarah's story, she also reveals more of the internal family dynamics that had preceded her mother's death. Six years after Sarah's banishment, Zora, back at home after her own time in exile, engages in a battle royal with Mattie. According to Hurston, she was driven by a fury that had been building up over the years and she unleashed that fury as she beat the woman almost senseless, feeling at the end that the beating had only made up for two of the six years that she had endured the woman's slights. Mattie insisted (to no avail) that Zora be arrested; not long after, the marriage between Mattie and John Hurston ended in divorce.

Having wandered off on a tangent about the effects her father's marriage had on Sarah, Hurston returns to the story of her schooling in Jacksonville six years earlier. She shares information about her unrequited crush on the school president and recalls her father's attempted abandonment by refusing to pay her school costs, suggesting that the school simply keep her. A school official had to advance the money for Zora's return home; once there, Zora found that the household had changed for the worse. She was outraged to find that Mattie Moge had taken Lucy's featherbed for herself, and Zora led a futile charge to reclaim her mother's bed. Gradually, each child either left home or was placed with someone, and Zora realized her visions of abandonment and homelessness.

Chapter 8, "Back Stage and the Railroad," is one of the longest chapters. Hurston uses the space to fill in details about her life between the time she was first forced to leave her childhood home (which she suggests was around the age of 10) until she arrived in Baltimore, Maryland, and was able to continue her formal education. Hurston tells us that during her early period of homelessness, she initially lived with a series of friends and relatives, attending school infrequently. She recalls it as a time of misery and lack, a time when she was expected to show humility, when she was reminded that she was fortunate to have food and shelter. Eventually, she sought out work as a domestic, but tended to fail at such jobs because she always managed to "get tangled up with their [her employers'] reading matter." Also, she was simply "not interested in dusting and dishwashing."[27] She provides a detailed account of one memorable position that primarily involved entertaining two little girls and from which she was summarily fired when the husband suspected that all her time with the children left his beautiful wife with too much free time on her hands. At another position, the husband propositioned her and Zora made the mistake of telling the wife about it. She lost that job and several others before accepting an invitation from her brother Dick to come to Sanford to live with his family. At that point, Zora's father insisted that she move into his house, which she found only a shell of the home it had once been. Her father, she felt, was a wreck with his "foundations rotted from under him."[28] Hurston stayed with her father and Mattie only a short period before moving on to another town to look for work.

During her wanderings, she stumbled across a copy of Milton's *Paradise Lost*, which she loved so much that she shirked her job-hunting duties in order to savor Milton's words. Around this time she found a temporary job in a doctor's office that might have turned permanent had not family intervened again. Her brother Bob asked her to come and live with his family, falsely promising her the chance to again attend school. She describes her situation in her brother's home as little more than that of an unpaid servant. Hurston tells us that her next job, which a poor white friend helped her secure, was that of lady's maid for an actor/singer in a Gilbert and Sullivan troupe. The balance of the long chapter is filled with her time traveling with the troupe, a time she looks back on with pleasure: "Before this job I had been lonely; I had been bare and bony of comfort and love. Working with these people I had been sitting by a warm fire for a year and a half and gotten used to the feel of peace."[29] Though she had been the butt of racial jokes, members of the troupe had poked fun at her southern way of speaking, and the pay she received for performing her job did not come close to what she had been promised, she had acquired a good informal education during her eighteen months with them. Her employer, whom she refers to as Miss M____ had even paid for a manicure course that would serve her well in the time ahead.

The end of the Gilbert and Sullivan job found Hurston in the Baltimore, Maryland, area looking for work. Though she was essentially without funds, she tells us that she was not bitter about not having received the pay that Miss M____ had promised her. She found work waiting tables, had to take time out to have her appendix removed, found another job and another after that, and yet another. She realized that she was "jumping up and down" in her own foot-tracks, and she sorely wanted to acquire more formal education. She entered night school where she met Dwight O. W. Holmes, whom she described as an amazingly dynamic teacher. His supportive words to her helped her muster the courage to sign up for Morgan College's high school department. Dean William Pickens credited her with two years of high school and assisted in finding her a live-in position in the home of a white clergyman, Dr. Baldwin. The Baldwins had a "great library," and Hurston tells us she "waded in," committing entire volumes to memory.[30]

At school, she was treated well by her economically superior classmates who were from "Baltimore's best Negro families."[31] Here, Hurston dallies to describe her good-looking, well-groomed classmates in great contrast to herself, but she also reminds the reader that she was naturally bright. She performed well in most of her classes and even took over for her teachers when they could not be there. Because she was such an outstanding student, Mae Miller – the daughter of a Howard University professor and future playwright – suggested that she apply at Howard. Hurston made the move to Washington, DC, that summer and subsequently worked as a waitress and manicurist to earn the money for tuition. The remainder of the chapter recounts Hurston's experiences at Howard and in Washington, including a specific incident in which a black man tried to get service at the whites-only shop where she worked as manicurist. Ultimately, the man was evicted from the shop and Hurston admitted to being as relieved as the other black workers who saw the man's attempt to challenge Jim Crow as a threat to their livelihood.

At Howard, Hurston joined the staff of the literary magazine, *Stylus*, which published her first short story, "John Redding Goes to Sea." Her affiliation with *Stylus* also brought her in contact with more established authors such as Georgia Douglas Johnson and others who frequented Johnson's literary salons. She explains how her short story in *Stylus* eventually brought her to the attention of Charles S. Johnson, founding editor of *Opportunity Magazine*. Not long after, Hurston moved to New York in January 1925 with a dollar and fifty cents, "no job, no friends, and a lot of hope."[32] At the first *Opportunity* awards dinner that May, she met several people who would have a profound impact on her future: novelist Fannie Hurst; Annie Nathan Meyer, a founder of Barnard College; and author Carl Van Vechten. Hurst would hire her as a secretary and later as a chauffeur/assistant, Meyer helped Hurston get into Barnard, and Van Vechten had connections in the publishing industry that would prove valuable to Hurston. At Barnard, Hurston maintained a "B" average and, as the school's only black student, became something of a *cause célèbre*. She also came to the attention of Columbia University's famous anthropologist, Franz Boas, and it was with his support that she did her first field work in collecting folklore. The chapter ends with her in the south beginning her first anthropological research, after stopping for a brief reunion with her family.

Chapter 10 is aptly titled "Research," which Hurston defines as "formalized curiosity . . . poking and prying with a purpose."[33] She confesses that she failed in her first attempt at conducting research into folk traditions because she approached her subject people as an outsider. When she returned, she approached them as an insider, living among them and essentially becoming one of them; her new approach proved much more successful. Sample tales from her fieldwork flesh out the chapter. She also recounts a personal story about narrowly escaping death at the hands of a jealous woman; she was saved because she had the foresight to befriend the toughest, most respected woman in that particular work settlement: Big Sweet. The story of that encounter is included in the text of *Mules and Men*. Hurston tells us that in addition to collecting the folk tales that would result in the publication of *Mules and Men*, she studied Hoodoo in New Orleans, traveled to Florida, and then went on to the Bahamas to collect music, and songs that she would later use to produce a revue. The chapter contains numerous details about Bahamian politics, as well as her travels in Haiti and Jamaica collecting information about Voodoo for *Tell My Horse*.

Hurston begins chapter 11 by recalling her idea for *Jonah's Gourd Vine*, when it came to her, and what she wanted the book to do. Here, she expresses her disdain at the thought of joining the herd of black authors writing about the "Race Problem"; she preferred to write about "what makes a man or a woman do such-and-so, regardless of his color."[34] In other words, she wanted to tell a story with universal implications. Feeling that no one expected her to tell a story that was not about the race problem, she put off writing her first novel for several years, and it was not until she published "The Gilded Six Bits" in *Story* that she came to the attention of Bertram Lippincott, whose company, J. B. Lippincott, would publish six of her seven books. The relationship turned out to be both blessing and curse because of the amount of control Lippincott sometimes exercised (or didn't exercise, as in the case of *Tell My Horse*) over her manuscripts. Hurston rented a house in Sanford (near Eatonville) and wrote *Jonah's Gourd Vine*, mailing the manuscript on October 3, 1933 and receiving an acceptance (with a $200 advance) on October 16, 1933. Interestingly, she compares the thrill of receiving her first acceptance and advance with the thrill of finding her first pubic hair.

Hurston had been trying for several years to organize her field notes into a publishable manuscript for *Mules and Men*, while working on other projects, including a concert for the Seminole County Chamber of Commerce. She proceeds hastily through the next eight years of her life, mentioning her studio work for Paramount, her travels in the Caribbean (to collect material for *Tell My Horse*), writing *Their Eyes Were Watching God* in Haiti (when she was supposed to be conducting research), and ending finally in California at the home of wealthy associate Katharane Edson Mershon working on *Dust Tracks on a Road.* She does not mention the publication of *Tell My Horse* in 1938 and *Moses, Man of the Mountain* in 1939; interestingly, she expresses a general lack of satisfaction with all her books.

The 1995 Library of America edition of Hurston's autobiography contains two versions of the essay "My People! My People!": the version included in the 1942 Lippincott edition as chapter 12 and an earlier version included – along with other material excised from the 1942 edition – as the Appendix. In chapter 12, Hurston explains that the title expresses the frustration and disdain a sophisticated, well-educated, well-dressed black person feels upon encountering black people of lesser class whose "trashiness" remains the standard by which all black people will be judged. The chapter is little more than an expository essay that offers the author's observations and opinions on intra-racial class prejudice, race pride, race consciousness, race prejudice, and other matters. She takes race leaders to task and argues that black people's interests are too varied for there to be such a thing as unity among them. Here, she displays her staunch individualism and her basic belief in self-determination. The highly unflattering essay points to hypocrisy after hypocrisy and inconsistency after inconsistency among black people who think that bonding along racial lines will assist the struggle for equal opportunity access in America. Hurston emphasized individual merit and achievement over collective racial enterprises throughout her autobiography and in much of her other work – always advancing the notion of the individual. The position did nothing to endear her to a growing chorus of black and white leftist critics.

Chapter 13 contains details of Hurston's relationships with novelist Fanny Hurst and singer/actor Ethel Waters. The stories about Hurst are fraught with ambiguity and deal mostly with the tricks she used to play on Hurston while she functioned as Hurst's assistant/chauffeur/confidante. The tone is matter of fact, the facts related in a very straightforward, unadorned manner. The section on Waters is more biographical; its tone is warmly analytical and reveals Hurston's deep affection for Waters. In chapter 14, Hurston discusses her experiences with love and the opposite sex from the time she was a young girl. She recalls her first grown-up love affair and subsequent marriage to Albert Price without mentioning Price by name. In very brief form and vague terms, she recalls the problems in their marriage, their divorce and his remarriage, her return to work, and meeting the next man with the initials PMP, for Percival M. Punter. Punter was the son of West Indian parents who was almost a generation younger than Hurston and, at the time, working on his master's degree at Columbia University. While Price had been a talented musician who went on to medical school to become a doctor, Punter was obviously a man of modest means with very strongly held traditional notions of marriage. Hurston describes the relationship as somewhat obsessive in nature. He clearly adored her and she was "hog-tied and branded." When his obsession took on a violent tone, she did not even respond as she might have had she not been so obsessed with him. According to Hurston, he was a magnificent physical specimen and his idea of being a man meant that he would take care of her in all ways, especially financially. The idea at first appealed to Hurston, but when he insisted that her work take a back seat to her role as his woman, the relationship was doomed. Still, Hurston recalls her time with him as the "real love affair" of her life.[35] The nature of the relationship is captured in the following words:

> But no matter how soaked we were in ecstasy, the telephone or the door bell would ring, and there would be my career again. A charge had been laid upon me and I must follow the call. He said once with pathos in his voice, that at times he could not feel my presence. My real self had escaped him. I could tell from both his face and his voice that it hurt him terribly. It hurt me just as much to see him hurt. He really had nothing to worry about, but I could not make him see it. So there we were. Caught in a fiendish trap. We could not leave each other alone, and we could not shield each other from hurt. Our bitterest enemies could not have contrived more exquisite torture for us.[36]

Hurston received a Guggenheim fellowship around this time and simply left without a word for the Caribbean, where she would "embalm all the tenderness" of her passion for him in the love affair between Janie and Tea Cake in *Their Eyes Were Watching God*. Two years later, she returned to New York and resumed her relationship with Punter, and thus it was ongoing while she was writing her autobiography. She expresses satisfaction in knowing that she had loved and "been loved by the perfect man." She had known "the real thing."[37] Having discussed the "real thing," Hurston goes on to discuss lesser affairs and fleeting romances that fulfill temporary needs and desires but are not substantial enough to come close to what she experienced with Punter. She ends by admonishing the reader not to take her thoughts on love as "gospel," for they are based solely on her own experiences. The playful two-line poem at the end seconds her admonition.

Hurston reveals her feelings about organized religion in chapter 15, titled "Religion." She deconstructs religious practice as she has witnessed it in much the same way that she deconstructs the idea of racial unity in "My People! My People!" She recalls growing up as a preacher's child and the questions she always had about God and religion from the time she was very young. She concludes with several questions and an assertion: "Why fear? The stuff of my being is matter, ever changing, ever moving, but never lost; so what need of denominations and creeds to deny myself the comfort of all my fellow men?

The wide belt of the universe has no need for finger-rings. I am one with the infinite and need no other assurance."[38]

Hurston begins her summary in the next chapter, "Looking Things Over." She reflects on her life up to that point, noting its peaks and valleys. She reiterates her dislike of bitterness, calling it the "under-arm odor of wishful weakness . . . the graceless acknowledgment of defeat." She credits her sense of humor with saving herself from personal, racial, or national arrogance, and she comments on human nature and the desire that keeps us from realizing universal justice. Echoing the sentiment of Booker T. Washington in *Up from Slavery*, she asserts that she sees no point in harboring bitterness about the history of slavery: "From what I can learn, it was sad. Certainly. But my ancestors who lived and died in it are dead. The white men who profited by their labor and lives are dead also. I have no personal memory of those times, nor no responsibility for them. Neither has the grandson of the man who held my folks." She proffers a definition of slavery that transcends the boundaries of the legal institution that ended in America after the Civil War: "Real slavery is couched in the desire and the efforts of any man or community to live and advance their interests at the expense of the lives and interests of others." She ends by extending her right hand of fellowship to the entire human race and imagining that after a few hundred generations it might indeed "breed a noble world."[39]

## Analysis

One simple definition for "autobiography" is the construction of the private self for public consumption, which helps to explain why Hurston was reluctant to write her autobiography: she was weary of being "devoured" by critics. African American autobiography comprises a unique subgenre of African American literature. The earliest examples include colonial or antebellum narratives about the experience of New World slavery, with perhaps the most recognizable of these being *The Interesting Narrative of Olaudah Equiano* (1789), *Narrative of the Life of Frederick Douglass, Written by Himself* (1845) and *Incidents in the Life of a Slave Girl* (1861) – though there are many others. The aforementioned autobiographical work by Booker T. Washington, *Up from Slavery*, is one of the most famous post-slavery works. Like Washington, Hurston set about making her autobiography different, unique, and individual. Like Washington, she managed to provide a record of damning evidence simply by laying out without analysis or judgment the details of certain experiences. Still, Hurston's representation of her life story diverges strongly from Washington's pragmatic rags to riches tale. Having endured the wrath and harsh criticism of the black literary establishment and white leftist critics for much of the previous decade,

Hurston went even further than Washington's evasiveness and ambiguity and presented to reading audiences a self that was more figurative than literal, a chameleon-like figure whose identity seemed irreducible. Compared to the heroic self that emerges in Washington's narrative, the partially obscured self that emerges from Hurston's pastiche-like volume is almost cosmic.

The work is, in fact, more memoir than conventional autobiography. Rather than providing an account of her life story from beginning to end, Hurston focuses on specific moments, events, and people and leaves the reader with an impressionistic rendering of the individual that is Zora Neale Hurston. Some critics read that individual in a favorable light; others do not. Interpretations vary based on the experiences, ideological influences, and beliefs of the readers. Her most strongly negative early reviews came from leftist white critics and male members of the black literary establishment, including Sterling Brown, Arna Bontemps, Alain Locke, and, later, Darwin Turner. For them, the volume was no doubt reminiscent of the accommodationist tone established by Washington in *Up from Slavery*, an unfortunate situation that only served to further alienate her from the black literary establishment and marginalize her work. For several critics, the 1942 Lippincott edition of *Dust Tracks on a Road* simply proved once and for all that Hurston was a sellout, a woman willing to do anything to get her work into print.

The first edition of *Dust Tracks on a Road* reveals more than anything else both her lack of agency as a black woman writer – subject to the mandates of a white-controlled publishing industry targeting a largely white American reading audience – and her substantial skill at maneuvering between the proverbial rock and a hard place. In addition to the compromises Hurston had to make in terms of content, *Dust Tracks on a Road* is filled with vagary and ambiguity, which only complicated matters for some critics who suggested that the volume was little more than fiction. For example, Hurston lists her birthplace as Eatonville, Florida, and seems not to know exactly when she was born. The lack of information immediately raises certain questions, and once again recalls Washington's narrative in which he also waxed duplicitous about the actual date of his birth. If Hurston's family was comparatively prosperous in Eatonville, as Hurston describes in the chapter preceding the one about her birth, why was the white man who assisted her mother in birth bringing them food? Since she was actually born in Notasulga, Alabama, how is it that she continues her relationship with the same white man years later in Eatonville? Did Lucy Potts Hurston die when Zora was 9 years old, or when she was closer to 13? Might a 13-year-old be more appropriately asked to do the things that a dying Lucy purportedly requested of Zora? Does Zora go off to school in Jacksonville at age 9 or age 13? Such questions reflect minor concerns surrounding the actual date of Hurston's birth, which we know to be January 7, 1891. Critics called Hurston on her lies and evasiveness, referring to her autobiography as fiction.

Contemporary readers and critics benefit from the research that scholars have conducted into the background of the text's production, including Hurston's initial drafts and the press editors' suggestions and directions for revision. By the time the manuscript came to print, it had gone through many changes and revisions that resulted in a representation of Hurston that was soothing to much of its white American readership, and discouraging to much of its black readership. The version of *Dust Tracks on a Road* that Lippincott released in 1942 was shaped to target a largely white readership. When Hurston donated her papers to the James Weldon Johnson Collection at Yale's Beinecke Rare Book and Manuscript Library, she included a note at the bottom of the title page accompanying a complete version of the manuscript for *Dust Tracks on a Road* which reads, "Parts of this manuscript were not used in the final composition of the book for publisher's reasons." Lippincott had excised, or reduced and dispersed through other sections of the manuscript, several sections: "Seeing the World as It Is," "The Inside Light – Being a Salute to Friendship," and "Concert"; the volume included a somewhat different version of "My People! My People!" New releases of *Dust Tracks on a Road* in the late twentieth century appended or restored the excised and/or dispersed material. Draft manuscripts reveal that Hurston was forced time and again to change her own words and perspectives on topics from race and politics in general, to the American military presence in developing nations and global imperialism – particularly after the bombing of Pearl Harbor and America's entry into World War II.

A surface reading of the first edition of *Dust Tracks on a Road* suggests a woman with almost no race consciousness; however, a closer examination even of the original published edition shows that Hurston delighted in and celebrated black culture and black consciousness on both personal and professional levels. Also, if we subject the chapter about friendships with Fannie Hurst and Ethel Waters to a close reading, we come away with the idea that the relationship with Hurst was more of the nature of the Pet Negro kind than the real friendship she shared with Ethel Waters. Hurston describes the cruel practical jokes she endured in her relationship with Hurst, while characterizing her relationship with Waters as warm and nurturing. And, while Lippincott allowed Hurston to articulate her belief in the universal nature of human experience, she could not add what she understood incisively: that one arrives at the universal only through an experience of the specific. Much of Hurston's personal and professional life up to that time had been spent celebrating the specificity and uniqueness of black culture in the United States, the Caribbean, and (by proxy) Africa. Her other writings, and particularly her last published novel, reveal that she was also very knowledgeable of white American culture and consciousness.

Faced with the task of revealing the details of her life under less than favorable conditions, asked to reveal "that which the soul lives by," Hurston offered the prototypical African American "featherbed resistance," which she describes in *Mules and Men*:

> The Negro, in spite of his open-faced laughter, his seeming acquiescence, is particularly evasive. You see we are a polite people and we do not say to our questioner, "Get out of here!" We smile and tell him or her something that satisfies the white person because, knowing so little about us, he doesn't know what he is missing. The Indian resists curiosity by a stony silence. The Negro offers a feather-bed resistance. That is, we let the probe enter, but it never comes out. It gets smothered under a lot of laughter and pleasantries.
>
> The theory behind our tactics: "The white man is always trying to know into somebody else's business. All right, I'll set something outside the door of my mind for him to play with and handle. He can read my writing but he sho' can't read my mind. I'll put this play toy in his hand, and he will seize it and go away. Then I'll say my say and sing my song."[40]

One wonders, nevertheless, whether there were times when Hurston stopped wearing her mask and it started wearing *her*. When does one become lost in her own duplicity? What were the paradoxes she faced and how does her autobiography reveal the different aspects of her personality? The mythic self that emerges from Hurston's work is gifted and hardworking, a staunch individualist and intellectual who desires the best that her country can offer its artists in bloom and its citizens in general. While the volume is truly unfortunate in a number of ways, its presence marks the compromises Hurston felt she had to make in order to get her work into print and still preserve something of her privacy. That fact alone makes it a valuable contribution to our understanding of American history and culture.

## *Seraph on the Suwanee* (1948)

### *Time period and setting*

The linear narrative proceeds from the third-person perspective, and the story begins just after the turn of the twentieth century in the backwoods west Florida town of Sawley on the Suwanee River, where the chief source of livelihood is the turpentine industry. We follow primary characters Arvay Henson Meserve and her husband Jim from Sawley to the town of Citrabelle, where fruit groves serve as the primary industry. The Meserves reside in Citrabelle for some twenty years, though Arvay makes trips home for family business and, near the end of the narrative, Jim leaves Arvay and moves to New Smyrna, Florida, the base for his shrimping business. Still, most of the story unfolds in and around Citrabelle and the nearby Great Swamp. Jim and Arvay's reconciliation takes place onboard the *Arvay Henson*, one of Jim's shrimping vessels. Each change of setting marks a positive change in Jim's and Arvay's economic prosperity.

## Major characters

Much of the narrative is filtered through Arvay Henson Meserve's consciousness. Arvay is introduced as a young, thin, blond "Florida cracker" with a natural talent for music. We soon learn that Arvay suffers from psychological and emotional wounds inflicted years before when her older (and, Arvay believes, favored) sister Larraine married Carl Middleton, the minister at their church. As church organist Arvay had worked closely with Middleton, and the two had developed feelings for each other; however, instead of approaching Arvay directly, Middleton made the mistake of attempting to use Larraine as a mediator and ended up married for life to the sister he did not want. Already suffering from an inferiority complex as a petite blonde in a community of voluptuous brunettes, Arvay believes Carl has deliberately and maliciously led her on. She develops a strange habit of throwing a fit to discourage suitors, believing that she will only end up suffering the same kind of humiliation she feels Carl inflicted on her. Jim Meserve sees through her act, however. To Arvay's surprise Jim marries her. A religious literalist, Arvay lacks an appreciation for nuance and is more often the butt of jokes than the one enjoying them. She goes through the motions of being a good wife as their fortunes increase over the years, but her transformation from passive participant to active subject does not take place until close to the end of the narrative.

Larraine Henson Middleton is Arvay's disloyal sister. Older, bigger, and brunette Larraine steals Carl Middleton, marries him despite knowing that it was Arvay he wanted, and essentially lives the life of a fat, unhappy house-wife who never forgets that Arvay was the sister that Carl really wanted. Brock and Maria Henson are Arvay and Larraine's proud and proper parents. Brock earns the family's humble living by working as a supervisor in the turpentine industry. Maria is in charge of hearth and home. On her deathbed she makes it known that she wants Arvay to inherit the family homestead, a bequest that angers Larraine and Carl.

Carl Middleton is the minister at the Henson family's church in Sawley, where he worked closely with teenaged Arvay, the church's young organist. He becomes enamored of her, but rather than approach her directly, he asks her older, bigger sister Larraine to intervene on his behalf. Larraine tricks him into believing that Arvay is not interested, and Carl ends up married to selfish and devious Larraine; the marriage brings out the worst in ambitionless Carl. He and Larraine live an unhappy hand-to-mouth, married-with-children existence. After Arvay becomes a married woman of means, they try to extract money from her.

Jim Meserve is the good-looking, dark Irish property-less descendant of people who owned plantations and slaves before the Civil War; he becomes wealthy over the course of the narrative. Carl Middleton's antithesis, Jim is anything but average; his overall demeanor reflects his southern aristocratic heritage, though his easy-going, affable nature wins him many strong associations across racial lines. Described as very attractive and highly desired by Sawley women, Jim's chauvinism is hard to miss. He courts a surprised Arvay, forces her to have sex with him, and then marries her. They have three children: the physically and mentally challenged Earl, the beautiful and outgoing Angeline, and the equally attractive and outgoing Kenneth.

Joe Kelsey is a black man who works at the Sawley area turpentine camp where Jim and Arvay settle initially. Joe and wife Dessie become close associates of the Meserves, achieving a status that is more than the employees they are, but less than that of intimate white friends. Indeed, the relationship between Jim and the Kelseys is reminiscent of "the pet Negro syndrome," which Hurston describes in her essay of the same name. To a lesser degree, the next generation of Kelseys will share a similar relationship with the Meserves. After the Meserves move from Sawley to Citrabelle, the Kelseys are invited to join them – to live and work on their property. Joe also runs a still for Jim, an enterprise that contributes a great deal to Jim's growing wealth. In contrast to the Meserves, the Kelseys never accumulate wealth; the narrator suggests stereotypically that they simply lack the capacity to manage money. The Meserves replace the Kelseys after Arvay learns about Jim's still (and Joe's part in it); believing that Joe is driving her husband's liquor business, she insists that the Kelseys leave, and they move to the Colored Town section of Citrabelle. The Kelsey children are Jeff and Belinda.

Alfredo Corregio is a Portuguese fisherman who teaches Jim Meserve the shrimping business. His wife, referred to as Mrs. Corregio, is described as a "Georgia cracker." The couple has two extremely beautiful daughters: Lucy Ann and Felicia. Older sister Lucy Ann's major role in the narrative is to serve as the victim of an attempted rape by Earl Meserve, whose instincts are closer to animal than human. Felicia will develop into a beautiful young woman and potential love interest for Kenneth Meserve.

## The surface story

*Seraph on the Suwanee* is presented as a love story, a romance about a psychologically repressed and emotionally underdeveloped woman and her chauvinist but loving and prosperous husband. Blonde, thin Arvay Henson is an anomaly among the other women of Sawley, Florida, including her sister Larraine. The narrator tells us that Arvay grew up with an inferiority complex, feeling that her parents favored her larger, more robust-looking sibling. When sister Larraine married Carl Middleton, who was the object of Arvay's affections, Arvay retreated even further into herself. The attention starved teenager had fallen easily for the somewhat older man who praised her natural musical ability. Arvay believes that Carl had deliberately led her on and made a fool of her, though Carl had merely been a victim of Larraine's duplicity. A heartbroken Arvay declares dramatically her intent to withdraw from the world and become a missionary in a far-off land. The Carl and Larraine incident caused her to distrust men's intentions in general, so much so that when young Sawley men persisted in their attempts to court her, she developed the routine of throwing a fit. She was thus labeled as weird, strange, or odd.

Several years pass before energetic and aggressive, hardworking and industrious Jim Meserve comes to Sawley. Jim's plan is to use whatever resources are at his disposal to realize the American Dream. Like other Sawley men, he appreciates Arvay's blonde, slender-but-shapely beauty – her difference from the typical Sawley maiden; he begins to keep company with her. Arvay's inferiority complex and her prior bad experience with Carl make it difficult for her to believe that Jim prefers her. She believes he is out to make a fool of her; when she goes into her usual fit, however, Jim is not so easily discouraged as her other suitors had been. As outgoing and gregarious as Arvay is withdrawn and reclusive, Jim sees through her faked fit and deliberately drops turpentine into her eye. Arvay's efforts to calm the ensuing eyeburn effectively end the charade, and the courtship proceeds.

Having dispensed with Arvay's primary mode of physical resistance to the courtship, Jim is nevertheless perplexed by her passive acquiescence and consults Joe Kelsey about how to make her a more active participant in the courtship. Joe advises him to take more aggressive action – "to break her and ride her hard" – whereupon Jim engages Arvay in forced sexual intercourse under her beloved mulberry tree. The rape ends with Arvay experiencing a mixture of pain and pleasure; she understands that she has two options at that point: marriage or ruin. She goes along with Jim's directive that they elope, and Arvay feels fortunate to have won a man so highly desired by other women. They set up their home near the turpentine camp where Jim works as a supervisor and Arvay goes through the motions of being a proper wife and homemaker. Arvay's personal psychological problems, including feelings of inadequacy and inferiority, continue to stifle her self-development for some twenty years of marriage. For many years, she continues to fantasize about Carl Middleton and, because she is something of a biblical literalist, judges herself harshly. When her first child, Earl, is born physically and mentally challenged, she believes that God is punishing her for mental adultery. Jim rejects Earl from the very beginning, declining even to participate in choosing a name for him. Though Arvay does her best to nurture Earl, she feels he represents her own personal failure.

In the meantime, Jim saves enough money to purchase five acres of land adjacent to a swamp near Citrabelle. Jim moves the family to their new home and learns all he can about growing fruit; he plants fruit groves with the help of local laborers. Arvay fears that her mentally challenged son will wander into the swamp and get lost, but as it turns out, Earl is at home in the swamp. In time, Arvay gives birth to two healthy children: first, a daughter, Angeline, described as beautiful, willful, and the apple of her father's eye; and a second son named Kenneth, who is as affable as his father and possesses his mother's natural talent for music. Jim's planning, shrewdness, and hard work propel the Meserves up the economic ladder in Citrabelle. He persuades Joe and Dessie Kelsey to move from Sawley to Citrabelle into a home on the Meserve property. Joe and Jim both make money in Jim's moonshine business, while Dessie helps Arvay with the household chores.

Despite her marriage to an apparently loving husband who is an excellent provider, humorless Arvay continues to experience occasional bouts of insecurity. The narrator tells us that she has everything a woman could want and yet she still expresses displeasure about feeling left out. She identifies strongly with Earl and resents the way Jim ignores him while delighting in his other two children. When young Kenny innocently induces his young playmate Belinda Kelsey to perform topsy turvy *sans* underwear, Arvay is outraged, but Jim chides her for being too serious. When Arvay learns that much of their income for many years has come from the still that Joe Kelsey runs for Jim, she blames Joe for being a bad influence and is eventually successful in driving the Kelseys off their property. The Kelseys subsequently experience an economic downturn. Joe, who has earned a good deal of money in the still operation, spends the money recklessly. Dessie, no longer living in close proximity to Arvay and free from her duties as Arvay's domestic servant, seems to lose her inspiration for homemaking.

When Jim becomes interested in the shrimping business, he finds an expert in Alfred Corregio and brings the Corregio family into the Kelsey's former home on Meserve property. Arvay is not pleased, believing the Corregios to be foreigners. Though Mrs. Corregio is a "Georgia cracker," Arvay finds herself longing for smiling, obliging Dessie. Also, the narrator informs us that Arvay is jealous of the extraordinarily beautiful Lucy Ann Corregio (who is, like Earl, in her late teens) and Mrs. Corregio. The younger daughter, Felicia, is only 7 or 8 years old when they arrive at the Meserve place. Jim learns the shrimping business from Alfredo and, over time, purchases three shrimping vessels. The first he christens the *Arvay Henson*; Arvay will not become aware of the fact until some time later, toward the end of the narrative. The success of Jim's new venture once again underscores his business savvy; Alfredo's knowledge and skill add to Jim's growing coffers.

Though Arvay's love for son Earl seems to blind her to the fact of his heightening mental illness, Jim senses Earl's propensity toward violence and suggests having him institutionalized. Arvay objects vehemently but later takes her son to Sawley to live with and help her widowed mother. After a short time, however, she brings Earl back to Citrabelle. Not long after his return, Earl attacks Lucy Ann Corregio; the rape is manifested as animal-like sexual violence to Lucy Ann's body rather than genital penetration. Returning to the house after learning of the attack, Arvay is attacked by a frightened and desperate Earl. Wresting herself from his hands, she knows that a search party / lynch mob has formed and beseeches him to run and hide. The search party, which includes Alfredo and Jim, tracks Earl to the swamp; it is clear that the swamp is a very familiar place for Earl because he has situated himself in a location where he cannot easily be taken; he has also armed himself with a rifle and ammunition. When Jim tries to approach, Earl shoots at him and is in turn killed by the search party. Deeply upset, Arvay mourns her dead son and temporarily turns away from her husband. A month later, she returns to her husband's arms and tries to be a dutiful wife and mother.

Angeline and Kenny grow into healthy and vivacious young people; both seem to have their father's temperament. When Angeline begins dating a Yankee, Hatton Howland, Arvay's provincial nature is once again disturbed; she hopes the relationship will be short-lived. Once again, however, she is the last one to understand what's happening right under her nose. She seems unaware of her own daughter's precociousness; when she hears Hatton playfully suggest that Angeline makes him consider rape, Arvay actually takes steps to kill the

Yankee, but Jim intervenes before she can proceed. Jim's lighthearted attitude about the whole affair brings out Arvay's insecurity, much as it has on other occasions. When Angeline and Hatton elope, Arvay tries to make her peace by doing her best to prepare a little wedding reception. She learns later that Jim had actually assisted the couple by giving underage Angeline his written permission and even accompanying the couple. Always aware of Arvay's thoughts, the reader learns that once again Arvay felt left out of things like some kind of second-class citizen.

The years pass and Arvay continues to feel like the outsider in most situations, though her inferiority complex does not extend to her interactions with nonwhites. Finally, a series of events sets into motion a change in Arvay's emotional state. First, her husband tries to impress her by demonstrating his fearlessness with a large snake. When the snake almost kills him while Arvay stands by paralyzed and unable to help, Jeff Kelsey comes to the rescue. Jim sees Arvay's paralysis as a sort of culminating event in her long history of passive co-existence. He leaves her with the admonition that he will give her a year to grow up and become the woman he knows she can be. Shortly thereafter, Arvay travels back to Sawley for her mother's death and funeral. While there, she experiences a rebirth which is associated with the burning down of the family home and, thus, the history that has long fed her feelings of inferiority. She travels to New Smyrna where Jim has taken up residence and actively takes her place beside him, apparently coming into her own as a full partner in her marriage.

## Analysis

Throughout her writing career, Hurston wrote with a double tongue, performing a form of literary masking, in order to create a record that could be read in different ways by people of differing ideological persuasions. Readers, depending on their beliefs and the degree to which they were influenced by prevailing ideologies, read the evidence in different ways.

The narrative voice in *Seraph on the Suwanee* represents the dominant ideological perspective of that time period in postwar America. In effect, the reader is placed in a subject position that is, among other things, white, male, and privileged. The view the novel advances of women, particularly Arvay, the perspective on race relations, on black people, and even on the mentally retarded must all be attributed to that perspective. Readers should also consider that Sigmund Freud's psychoanalytic theories were immensely popular at the time, and the novel was written during the postwar period when many white women who had left hearth and home to enter the workplace were encouraged to return to the domestic sphere. America was on the cusp of the 1950s. Readers also must consider how the information in a given text is mediated; certainly, a careful reader does not simply accept the narrator's judgments and assessments as gospel. While the surface narrative showcases Hurston's desire to show that, regardless of skin color, human beings essentially want the same things out of life, a deeper understanding of the story reveals obvious signs of white privilege and entitlement that permeate the story. When we consider individual characters' words and actions along with the narrator's ideological biases, we come away with a very different understanding of the story than a surface reading allows.

For example, while some contemporaneous critics called attention to the "melting pot" aspect of the novel's characterization, contemporary readers will note that the white Meserve family is always at the top of the economic hierarchy. Combined race and class privilege guarantees them starring roles in their relationships with people of color, who serve supporting roles. At the Sawley area turpentine mill, Jim's class background and race afford him a position of authority in the hierarchy. Though Dessie Kelsey clearly has a home and family of her own, Arvay expects and receives her help with household chores. After Joe Kelsey teaches Kenny Meserve how to play black music, Kenny enthusiastically announces that he plans to do what other whites are doing with black music – take it over for the purpose of acquiring capital. In Kenny, we witness the merging of his mother's natural talent for music with his father's vision for capital gain; Hurston's publisher excised a chapter describing Kenny's financial success with black music. Hurston casts descendant of former slaveholders Jim Meserve as the most likeable, affable, and all-around self-actualized person in the novel. When Joe and Dessie Kelsey are in close proximity to him, they prosper and generally act like responsible human beings. When they are driven off the Meserve property, they seem to lose their focus and balance. Though we are reminded time and again of Jim Meserve's fairness, it is difficult to miss the fact that he develops his wealth through the deliberate (but friendly) exploitation of the labor and wisdom of people considered his racial and/or economic inferiors. Everyone works on his behalf in the modified antebellum arrangement, and he is perceived as the natural superior of white women and people of color. In addition, Jim rejects his own mentally challenged son; viewed through the lens of Hurston's suspect narrator, Earl is effectively "blackened" by his mental infirmity and, as such, submits to his animal instincts in the rape of Lucy Ann Corregio; the idea is reinforced by Earl's subsequent lynching.

While the narrator points to Arvay's psychological problems as the cause for all the problems in the marriage, Hurston includes ample evidence of Jim's thoughtless chauvinism as contributing to the problems in the marriage;

however, presented through the biased narrator, Jim is never judged as anything other than normal, while Arvay is deemed whiny, intolerant, and inadequate. The narrator even seems to want the reader to believe that somehow Arvay should have been able to prevent a snake from squeezing Jim to death! Jim's statements that women understand almost nothing and were created to feel and not to think, his pre-marital and post-marital rapes of Arvay, his blatant announcement that she is his property and must submit to him, and his general tendency not to share information with her are all evidence of his chauvinist, patriarchal vision of the world where he functions as neo-slavemaster. He also leaves his wife out of all his business dealings.

Arvay may enjoy a certain amount of white privilege, and her feelings of white superiority are evident, but she clearly feels inferior in her relationship with Jim. She muses that she is (sexually and otherwise) "like a slave" to Jim Meserve. Though Arvay is the protagonist in the story, she is a shadowy figure in her own life before her transformation; change occurs for her after Jim leaves her and her mother dies. Finally, she takes the time she needs to confront some truths about her life.

The title of the novel becomes most relevant during Arvay's transformative period and during the final trip to the family home on the Suwanee. Hurston finally settled on the title for *Seraph on the Suwanee* after considering a number of working titles, including "The Queen of the Golden Hand," "Sang the Suwanee in the Spring," "Lady Angel with Her Man," "Good Morning Sun," "Seraph with a Man on Hand," "Angel in the Bed," "So Said the Sea," and "Seraph on the Suwanee River." The word "seraph" is from the Hebrew word meaning "to burn"; in Isaiah 6:1–3, it refers to a certain order of protective angels with six wings. The passage reads in part that the sounds of the seraphim's voices moved the "foundations of the thresholds" of the Temple. In Numbers, the word is associated with a fiery or poisonous serpent, and here it is tempting to read the scene in which Jim is almost killed by the snake in combination with Arvay's subsequent burning of her old home on the Suwanee. In each case, foundations are destroyed. After the snake incident, Jim leaves the marriage, and after Arvay burns down her childhood home and the rats in its walls, she feels confident enough to take the time she needs to complete her journey of self-discovery before returning to the marriage as the woman of agency depicted in the final scenes of the novel. Her exercise of choice reflects a newfound freedom – that of realizing she has options. She returns to her marriage through a deliberate act and actively embraces her role in the relationship. While that role represents less than what many would see as a feminist ideal, it is nevertheless realistic in the same sense that Janie Crawford's less than ideal relationship with Tea Cake in *Their Eyes Were Watching God* could still be the love affair of her life.

In *Seraph on the Suwanee*, Hurston continues her concern with gender relations, focusing on a central heterosexual relationship such as that of Lucy and John in *Jonah's Gourd Vine*, and Janie and each of her three husbands in *Their Eyes Were Watching God*. Though she diverges from a central concern with a heterosexual liaison in *Moses, Man of the Mountain*, she remains focused on gender relations in that novel; and though she is concerned with bringing her protagonists to voice in each of the novels, John Pearson (as preacher in *Jonah's Gourd Vine*) and Moses (as leader of a people in *Moses, Man of the Mountain*) represent her best accomplishments in that regard. One must read far beneath the surface narrative, however, to uncover Hurston's critique of race relations in *Seraph on the Suwanee*. A more egalitarian racial dynamic is suggested through the Corregio marriage, the potential for a relationship between Kenneth Meserve and Felicia Corregio, and the multicultural scenario aboard the shrimping vessels near the end of the story. Such settings note the changing social climate in postwar America.

With *Seraph on the Suwanee*, Hurston no doubt wanted to illustrate a basic tenet of her overall philosophy that human beings are human beings, regardless of skin color. However, she also created a record of a skewed system that condones the forms of neo-slavery that existed in the United States many decades after the official end of slavery and continued to guarantee the best opportunities for economic success to white men. Still, she is careful to avoid assigning to her sympathetic black characters the kind of social determinism that plagued Richard Wright's Bigger Thomas in *Native Son* (1940). Her depictions of Joe and Dessie Kelsey in *Seraph on the Suwanee*, her depiction of John Pearson's reversal of fortunes in *Jonah's Gourd Vine*, her representation of the slave mentality that plagued the first and second generations of newly freed blacks in *Moses, Man of the Mountain*, all reflect her belief in personal responsibility and the idea that true freedom comes through self-knowledge. Hurston's belief that individuals, not groups, possessed the power to transcend the social and economic barriers associated with America's color line is also represented in her shorter works.

## Short stories

Between 1921 and the time of her death, Hurston published some eighteen short stories and a compilation of tales titled "The Eatonville Anthology." Seven previously unpublished stories have also come to light: "Black Death"; "The Bone of Contention"; "Book of Harlem"; "Harlem Slanguage"; "Now You Cookin' with Gas"; "The Seventh Veil"; and "The Woman in Gaul."[41] Hurston's fiction often reflected her intimate knowledge of folk culture, particularly the specific cultural environment from which she emerged in central Florida, but also the African diasporic cultures she encountered in her travels and fieldwork in anthropology. Her writings focused attention on basic human motivations and the issues that arise out of the everyday dynamics of human interactions. Her stories celebrate what she felt was the beauty and depth of the everyday interior lives of black people in the United States and in the Caribbean.

Hurston often used her short stories to examine gender dynamics and expectations, just as she did with her long fiction. As critic Wilfred Samuels has noted, Hurston's short stories, far from representing the author's apprentice work, actually served as the source material or the germ for her longer works. Indeed, in her first two short stories the actions of male and female protagonists validate the narrator's representation of gender differences in the opening lines of *Their Eyes Were Watching God*. Both somewhat autobiographical, "John Redding Goes to Sea" (May 1921) and "Drenched in Light" (December 1924), represent Hurston's early forays into the realm of gender dynamics. The primary issue in the life of her title character and protagonist in "John Redding," however, is his inability to act on his dream of going to sea – a metaphor for exploring the bounds of human potential for self-actualization. For young Isie Watts, the Hurston-like protagonist of "Drenched in Light," the central issue is the fact that she "hears a different drummer" and follows it despite warnings and admonitions from authority figures. Taken together, the protagonists from her two earliest stories exemplify the sentiment expressed by the narrator at the beginning of *Their Eyes Were Watching God*:

> Ships at a distance have every man's wish on board. For some they come in with the tide. For others they sail forever on the horizon, never out of sight, never landing until the Watcher turns his eyes away in resignation, his dreams mocked to death by Time. That is the life of men. Now, women forget all those things they don't want to remember, and remember everything they don't want to forget. The dream is the truth. Then they act and do things accordingly.[42]

As the title of the story suggests, John Redding dreams of going to sea to gain experience and self-knowledge. First his mother and then his wife prevent him from acting on his desire to travel, his mother Matty believing that a witch sprinkled travel dust on their doorstep the morning of John's birth to exact revenge on John's father Alfred for not marrying her daughter. Matty thus does everything in her power to thwart the effects of the spell by squelching John's dreams. As a child, the frustration (and ultimately the fate) that John will experience as an adult is reflected in a scene where his toy ships (actually twigs) fail to launch. His father warns him that such failures also happen to people. Nevertheless, John follows his mother's advice and marries rather than going to sea, stifling his desire for the "open road" and "rolling seas," and for the experience of unknown people and countries. Tragically and ironically, John is killed when he is washed from a bridge during a flood. In death he finally realizes his dream of going to sea. Matty and Alfred have seen the death coming in the doleful cry of a screech owl that lands on their roof, but their actions – Matty burns salt in a lamp and turns her bathrobe inside out, and Alfred turns his socks inside out – are not enough to prevent John's demise.

While "John Redding Goes to Sea" was a product of Hurston's undergraduate years at Howard University, "Drenched in Light" introduced her to the literary world of New York City. Protagonist, Isie Watts is remarkably similar to the young Zora Neale Hurston that emerges from subsequent writings, including *Dust Tracks on a Road*. As such, the story is an assertion of Hurston's personal identity and an affirmation of the special nurturing she experienced growing up. It tracks a day in Isie's life, in which the little girl sits upon the gatepost near the road that runs past her Eatonville, Florida, home for the purpose of greeting and interacting with travelers on the road to and from Orlando. The almost completely autobiographical story even includes a stern and disapproving grandmother who tries to stifle Isie's exuberance. It provides a glowing perspective on self-governing, all-black Eatonville as the source of the ebullient spirit exemplified by the highly self-confident dreamer, Isis, a perspective that will be greatly expanded in subsequent novels and short stories. The irrepressible Isie turns somersaults, dances, runs with the family dogs, and even tries to shave Grandma Potts' facial hair while the old woman is asleep. Isie's favorite activity, however, is engaging with the people who travel on the road past the gatepost where she waits, eager to perform for them or to secure a ride in their cars. Interestingly and perhaps problematically, Hurston casts Isie as the inspiration for a white woman named Helen whose life is empty and dead; upon witnessing Isie's performance of a gypsy dance, Helen feels the potential for her own renewal. On the pretext of exposing Isie to a more privileged existence, Helen spends time with Isie in order to gain greater exposure to what she has to offer. Drenched in light, Isie becomes the source of light for Helen's soul. "Drenched in Light," is simply one of the first of Hurston's many celebrations of rural southern black culture in her fiction. The story suggests black America possesses the tonic for what white America needs to revive its lackluster soul.

Between June 1925 and November 1926, Hurston published five more short stories, including "Spunk" (June 1925); "Magnolia Flower (July 1925); "Muttsy" (August 1926); "'Possum or Pig?" (September 1926); and "The

Eatonville Anthology" (September–November 1926). Hurston published four short stories during the 1940s: "Cock Robin Beale Street" (July 1941); "Story in Harlem Slang" (July 1942); "High John De Conquer" (October 1943); and "Hurricane" (1946), which was culled from the section from *Their Eyes Were Watching God* in which Tea Cake is bitten by a rabid dog following a hurricane, and Janie must kill him or be killed by him. During her final decade, Hurston published "Escape from Pharoah" (1950) and "The Tablets of the Law" (1951).

One of Hurston's most often anthologized short stories is "Spunk," which exemplifies her concern with gender dynamics, particularly how masculinity is constructed and asserted. While John Redding of *Jonah's Gourd Vine* offered a model of stifled masculinity, Spunk Banks represents society's notion of masculinity taken to the extreme. His physical stature, strength, and capacity for finessing the most difficult machinery at the mill are not enough; his feelings of masculine superiority are manifested in his public dating of Lena Kanty, whose husband Joe is both smaller in stature and less prideful and ego-driven. Still, Joe Kanty must follow the dictates of honor and manhood: he confronts Spunk with a pocket razor and is killed by Spunk's superior weapon, an army 45 gun.

After a brief trial, Spunk is free to take full, legal possession of Lena. Soon after, however, Spunk declares that he believes he is being hunted by Joe in the body of a black bobcat; later, as Spunk lies dying from a work-related injury, he swears it was Joe's spirit that pushed him into the machinery over which he had long proven his mastery. Spunk's pride had clearly been diminished before his fall (or push) into the saw. Hoodoo (which is used more explicitly as a medium for exacting revenge in Hurston's short story "Black Death") is implicit in this story as the source for Spunk's decline in prestige and demise alongside a growing myth of Joe's superior courage. The story ends with a suggestion that both men would have been better off had they never crossed paths with a woman like Lena. The final lines of the story underscore the male and female differences in reactions to Lena. Men desire her despite the fact that she has been complicit in the deaths of two men; women wonder who will be her next.

Gender again takes center stage in "Sweat" (November 1926). The setting is springtime in Eatonville, Florida, in the early 1900s; the primary characters are Delia and Sykes Jones, though the men who sit on the porch at Joe Clarke's store comment on Sykes's shallowness and make suggestions about how best to teach him a lesson. Delia and Sykes have been married for fifteen years and almost from the beginning Sykes has been a demanding and physically abusive husband to Delia; she is, on the other hand, a self-sacrificing, hardworking wife. Sykes wants to replace scrawny Delia with the most recent of his series of infidelities, the robust Bertha; however, he expects Delia to leave the home that she has paid for with her hard work as a washwoman. In addition to his philandering and physical abuse, Sykes berates Delia for taking in white folks' laundry, as her source of livelihood undermines his sense of manhood. Sykes knows that Delia, an ardent Christian, is profoundly fearful of snakes, so he tries to drive her away by placing a diamond back rattlesnake in a wooden soapbox near the kitchen door. Sykes leaves the snake in its box outside the kitchen door. Neighbors come by to see and comment on the snake, and Delia grows increasingly irate at its presence. Eventually, she vents her fury at Sykes, telling him she hates him and would be fine if he just left her alone. Sykes is caught off guard by Delia's highly uncharacteristic declaration of hatred and disdain for the marriage; he leaves and does not return that night.

The next day, Delia goes off to her Sunday evening church service as usual and, upon returning home full of the spirit, sets about her usual Sunday work of sorting laundry. As soon as she opens her hamper, she discovers the snake there where Sykes had placed it. Delia escapes to the barn and spends the night there in contemplation: "for an hour or more she lay sprawled upon the hay a gibbering wreck. Finally she grew quiet, and after that, coherent thought. With this, stalked through her a cold, bloody rage. Hours of this. A period of introspection, a space of retrospection, then a mixture of both. Out of this an awful calm."[43] When Sykes returns to a darkened house thinking Delia has been killed by the snake, the snake attacks him. He kills the snake but only after he has been bitten numerous times. Delia listens to the fierce altercation between Sykes and the snake, and she hears Sykes's cries for help; when she finally makes a move, she goes toward him only to retreat and listen while he dies knowing that she did nothing to save him from the venom that he had set loose on himself. He has been his own worst enemy.

Hurston's story offers a critique of blind religious faith via a twist on the biblical serpent-in-the-garden story, while addressing intra-racial gender relations and Jim Crow's barriers to equal opportunity access. Both Delia and Sykes are limited in terms of the kinds of employment available to them. The employment situation contributes to Sykes's weakened sense of manhood, which is evidenced by his womanizing tendencies. He is further chagrined by Delia's ability to endure his abuse while making a living taking in the white folks' dirty laundry, and even further by her ability to thrive independent of the financial contributions he withholds. While Delia's faith seems to drive her capacity for living, in reality her blind devotion to religion keeps her in the oppressive relationship. The careful reader will note that several unchristian acts set in motion the final series of events that result in her deliverance from the martyrdom that has characterized her fifteen years of marriage to the cruel Sykes. Delia's period of martyrdom ends when she behaves most unchristian-like – by expressing hatred, by voicing her desire for the marriage to end, and by allowing Sykes to die after the rattler bites him. From the period of introspection during her night in the barn, she emerges a profoundly changed person. Interestingly, the snake she calls "ol' satan" serves as her agent of deliverance.

During the next decade, Hurston published four more stories: "The Gilded Six Bits" (1933), the story that brought her to the attention of Bertram Lippincott who would publish all except one of her books; "Mother Catherine" (1934); "Uncle Monday" (1934); and "The Fire and the Cloud" (1934), which was the seed story for *Moses, Man of the Mountain*. "The Gilded Six Bits" is a story about a marital relationship that survives the wife's infidelity. The setting is Zora's Eatonville: "a Negro yard around a Negro house in a Negro settlement."[44] Joe and Missie May Banks are a happy couple; they have been married for a year when Joe discovers that Missie May has been unfaithful with the new businessman in town, Otis D. Slemmons. Slemmons wears what purports to be a five-dollar gold piece for a stick-pen and a ten-dollar gold piece on his watch chain. Missie May loves Joe dearly, and the two are loving and playful with each other, but she is taken in by Slemmons' promise to give her his gold. In fact, the two pieces together (a quarter and a fifty-cent piece painted gold) are worth only six bits; hence, the story's title. Missie May's betrayal makes Joe distant, and Missie May decides to leave her marital home. Her plans change when she encounters Joe's mother; she does not want to give the woman the satisfaction of seeing the marriage end. Months pass before Joe and Missie May manage a tentative reconciliation that finally becomes fully realized when Missie May gives birth to a son who looks like Joe. The story ends on the same note that it began – with Joe and Missie May engaged in a playful ritual: Joe comes home from work throwing coins on the floor for Missie May to harvest and add to their savings for the future.

"The Gilded Six Bits" diverges from other literary treatments of unfaithful women in that Missie May is depicted as a woman who makes a mistake for which she can be, and is, redeemed through the birth of her son. That Joe seems poised to forgive her even before his son is born speaks volumes about his character and his confidence in his own manhood. Readers will also notice the gender dynamic in the Banks household. Joe brings home the money and Missie May focuses on creating all the comforts of hearth and home when he arrives. She is the "perfect wife," as she reminds Joe, and she seems completely satisfied with the arrangement. Indeed, Missie May's devotion to Joe and to their marriage makes it difficult to believe that her infidelity is fed by a fixation on the ten-dollar gold piece that paunchy blowhard Otis D. Slemmons has promised her. Missie May clearly has access to more money than the two gold pieces combined would be worth, and she is equally as clearly not attracted to Slemmons. A deeper reading of the story suggests that Missie May, despite the fact of the silver dollars Joe brings home for their savings every week, desires some money of her own earned outside the confines of the marital relationship. That the means by which she hopes to obtain the money is foolhardy goes without saying, but the playful game she engages in with Joe every Saturday is its own kind of compromise for fulfilling her gendered role in the marriage. While her creative spirit manifests itself in the pleasing aesthetics of their colorful yard and the food she takes pride in serving her husband, Missie May's options for self-actualization beyond the confines of even this pleasant marriage are sorely limited in that time and place.

Hurston's evolution as a skilled crafter of short stories is evident in the increasing strength of her narratives. She continued to draw upon a wealth of materials to expose the intricacies of human emotions and relationships. She grew increasingly assured of her special expertise, exhibiting her mastery of the southern rural vernacular, as well as the folk traditions – including Hoodoo, and Voodoo – which she incorporates into her stories. While Hurston insisted on telling the stories she wanted to tell, she was also acutely aware of the significance of political context in telling those stories. Thus, she carefully weighed such factors as she crafted her work, and sometimes – as with her autobiography – the result was an ambiguous, almost chameleon-like document.

As part of Hurston's literary resurrection, scholars have added a number of posthumously published and edited volumes of her work. Alice Walker edited *I Love Myself When I Am Laughing . . . & Then Again When I Am Looking Mean and Impressive: A Zora Neale Hurston Reader* (1979), for the Feminist Press. The volume includes an extended dedication by Walker, an introduction by Mary Helen Washington, and selections from a number of Hurston's writings under three headings: "Autobiography, Folklore, and Reportage"; "Essays and Articles"; and "Fiction." Walker's afterword, "Looking for Zora," rounds out the volume. *The Sanctified Church* (1981) is a collection of Hurston's groundbreaking essays on African American folklore, legend, popular mythology, and the unique spiritual character of the southern black Christian church. Along with preserving the customs, speech, music, and humor of rural black America, the book introduces us to a number of interesting figures: Uncle Monday, a healer, conjurer, and powerful herb doctor; Mother Catherine, matriarchal founder of a Voodoo Christian sect; and High John the Conquerer, a trickster/shaman figure of freedom and laughter. The volume captures the exuberance, vitality, and genius of black culture with unmatched authority and vividness. Toni Cade Bambara provides the foreword for the collection, which includes sections titled "Herbs and Herb Doctors," "Characteristics of Negro Expression," "The

Sanctified Church," and "The Florida Observations." Other collected works include *Spunk: The Selected Short Stories of Zora Neale Hurston* (1985), *Mule Bone: A Comedy of Negro Life* (1991), *The Complete Stories* (1995), *Folklore, Memoirs, & Other Writings* (1995), *Novels and Stories* (1995), *Go Gator and Muddy the Water: Writings by Zora Neale Hurston from the Federal Writers' Project* (1999), and *Every Tongue Got to Confess: Negro Folk-Tales from the Gulf States* (2001).[45]

## Notes

1. Much critical work for the novel focuses on John's capacity for language and poetry in his role as black southern rural preacher.
2. *MAM*, in Wall, *Women of the Harlem Renaissance*, p. 176
3. *Hemenway, Zora Neale Hurston*, pp. 118–19.
4. See Daphne Lamothe, "Vodou Imagery, African American Tradition, and Cultural Transformation in Zora Neale Hurston's *Their Eyes Were Watching God*," in *Zora Neale Hurston: A Casebook*, ed. Cheryl Wall (New York: Oxford, 2000), pp. 165–87.
5. *TEWWG*, p. 11.
6. Ibid., p. 192.
7. Ibid., p. 171.
8. Ibid., pp. 32–3
9. Ibid., pp. 15–16.
10. Carla Kaplan, "The Erotics of Talk: 'That Oldest Human Longing'" (1995), in Wall, ed., *Zora Neale Hurston*, pp. 137–63.
11. Ibid., p. 20.
12. Ibid., p. 25.
13. Ibid., p. 26.
14. Ibid., pp. 39, 46, 49–50, 161.
15. Ibid., pp. 81–97.
16. Lamothe, "Vodou Imagery," p. 171.
17. *TMH*, p. 3.
18. Ibid., p. 19.
19. Ibid., p. 82.
20. *MMOTM*. (1939; Urbana and Chicago, IL: University of Illinois Press, 1984), p. 154.
21. See Lamothe, "Vodou Imagery."
22. *DTOAR*, p. 20.
23. Ibid., p. 28.
24. Ibid., p. 30.
25. Ibid., pp. 32, 43.
26. Ibid., p. 70.
27. Ibid., pp. 88, 89.

28. Ibid., p. 98.
29. Ibid., p. 119.
30. Ibid., pp. 122, 124.
31. Ibid., p. 125.
32. Ibid., p. 138.
33. Ibid., p. 143.
34. Ibid., p. 171.
35. Ibid., pp. 207, 208.
36. Ibid., p. 210.
37. Ibid., p. 212.
38. Ibid., p. 226.
39. Ibid., pp. 227, 229, 230, 232.
40. Hurston, "Introduction," *MAM*, in Wall, *Zora Neale Hurston*, p. 10.
41. All of Hurston's short stories are collected in Gates and Lemke, *Zora Neale Hurston*
42. *TEWWG*, p. 9.
43. "Sweat," (1926), in Gates and Lemke, *Zora Neale Hurston*, pp. 73–85.
44. "The Gilded Six Bits," (1933), in Gates and Lemke, *Zora Neale Hurston*, pp. 86–98.
45. Walker, *I Love Myself When I Am Laughing; The Sanctified Church*, fwd. Toni Cade
    Bambara (Berkeley, CA: Turtle Island Foundation, 1981); *Spunk: The Selected Short
    Stories of Zora Neale Hurston* (Berkeley, CA: Turtle Island Foundation, 1985); *Mule
    Bone: A Comedy of Negro Life*, eds. George Houston Bass, Henry Louis Gates, Jr.
    (New York: HarperPerennial, 1991); Gates and Lemke, *Zora Neale Hurston*; *Zora
    Neale Hurston: Novels and Stories*, ed. Cheryl Wall (New York: Library of America,
    1995); *Go Gator and Muddy the Water: Writings by Zora Neale Hurston from the
    Federal Writers' Project*, ed. Pamela Bordelon (New York: W. W. Norton, 1999); and
    *Every Tongue Got to Confess: Negro Folk-Tales from the Gulf States*, ed. Carla Kaplan
    (New York: HarperCollins, 2001).

# Critical reception

This chapter provides an overview of how Hurston's work has been read and understood both during her life and since her literary resurrection in the 1970s. Zora Neale Hurston's somewhat mixed and often negative early critical reception has been a recurring issue in scholarship about her life and work. Critical reception of literary work is influenced by a number of variables, including the author's purpose for writing, target audience demographics, publishing industry guidelines, the prevailing socio-political order, the prevailing ideology or ideologies, plus internal modes of production that affect mediation – the manner in which the narrative is transmitted to the reader. Add to these variables the fact that Hurston, like other writers associated with the New Negro Movement, relied heavily on patronage that typically came with its own set of conditions. Finally, mainstream American literary criticism took little sustained notice of African American literature prior to the 1970s. Robert Hemenway's *Zora Neale Hurston: A Literary Biography* (1977), Valerie Boyd's *Wrapped in Rainbows: The Life of Zora Neale Hurston* (2003), and particularly M. Genevieve West's *Zora Neale Hurston and American Literary Culture* (2005), all allocate substantial space to examining contexts for contemporaneous criticism of Hurston's work, which helps in understanding some of the reasons that the author died in obscurity and why a literary resurrection was necessary. Still, one must not discount the writer's own personality and how she engages with, and responds to, each of the variables mentioned above.

Hurston's desire that her work serve as a vehicle for illuminating white America as to the innermost thoughts and emotions of black Americans no doubt played a role in the divergent forms (often along racial lines) that contemporaneous reviews of her work took on. In "What White Publishers Won't Print" (1950), she asserted her concern with limited representations of African Americans, noting that the "fact that there is no demand for incisive and full-dress stories around Negroes above the servant class is indicative of something of vast importance to this nation." Concerned about too much attention to the so-called "race problem" in literary representation, Hurston noted the following:

> But for the national welfare, it is urgent to realize that the minorities do think, and think about something other than the race problem. That they are very human and internally, according to natural endowment, are just like everybody else. So long as this is not conceived, there must remain that feeling of unsurmountable [*sic*] difference, and difference to the average man means something bad. If people were made right, they would be just like him.
>
> The trouble with the purely problem arguments is that they leave too much unknown. Argue all you will or may about injustice, but as long as the majority cannot conceive of a Negro or a Jew feeling and reacting inside just as they do, the majority will keep right on believing that people who do not feel like them cannot possibly feel as they do, and conform to the established pattern.[1]

In other words, Hurston felt that, by lifting the veil and revealing their everyday lives, the oppressed could make their oppressors more aware of their common humanity. Hurston's unwillingness to engage primarily in social protest (what she referred to in "How It Feels to Be Colored Me" as the "sobbing school of Negrohood"[2]) earned her the ire of a number of members of the black literary establishment, including Richard Wright, whose scathing October 1937 review of *Their Eyes Were Watching God* in "Between Laughter and Tears," is well known in literary circles. Her refusal to join the voices of social protest so prevalent during that time period, or even to join those who insisted that black people must always be presented in a favorable light, underscored the strong individualist spirit that had been evident since her youth. Her insistence upon celebrating the oral rural southern vernacular parallels Langston Hughes' insistence on creative freedom in his "The Negro Artist and the Racial Mountain" (1926); yet, there was something about Hurston's depiction of the folk that (generally speaking) simultaneously charmed white people and made black people nervous.[3]

From the perspective of the twenty-first century, it seems that in either case, the problem was centered on the critic rather than on the work (or author) under critique. For example, while *New York Times* critic Margaret Wallace called *Jonah's Gourd Vine* "the most vital and original novel about the American Negro that has yet been written by a member of the Negro race," Andrew Burris of *Crisis* described the work as "quite disappointing and a failure as a novel."[4] From a twenty-first-century perspective, one easily notes both the paternalistic tone of Wallace's review and the racial embarrassment that permeates Burris's critique. Indeed, among the black literary establishment, her work was often trivialized as entertainment, and minstrelsy, rather than serious literary achievement.

Regardless of race, early critics almost always missed both the nuance and the complexity of Hurston's work, including her critiques of gender role expectations and religion, her skill at ethnography, and even the autobiographical and biographical aspects of her writing that would become more apparent after she wrote her autobiography and after her literary resurrection. Though well-known critic Darwin Turner would offer a review of Hurston's literary career in his 1971 work, *In a Minor Chord*, it was author Alice Walker's early 1970s search for literary foremothers that has been largely credited with Hurston's resurrection. Robert Hemenway followed up with his definitive 1977 literary biography of Hurston.

Since Hurston's literary resurrection, scholars of black women's literature and black feminist and womanist thought have hailed her as an important link between nineteenth-century black women writers and those writing since 1950. She has also been championed by cultural anthropologists for her pioneering work in southern and Caribbean folk traditions. As scholarly attention increased, presses reintroduced Hurston's works, making them readily available to scholars and the general public. The number of book-length scholarly treatments of Hurston's work increases each year, allowing for new critical assessments of her work; however, reviews still serve as the primary sources for assessing contemporaneous criticism and reception of the seven book-length works she produced between 1934 and 1948. Contemporary criticism of Hurston's work focuses on her artistry in combination with her philosophy and on how her body of work has continuing relevance for English and Literary Studies, African American Studies, Womanist/Feminist/Gender Studies, Anthropology, and History.

## Jonah's Gourd Vine (1934)

By the time Hurston published *Jonah's Gourd Vine*, she was already an award-winning writer and a well-known folklorist and anthropologist. Contemporaneous reviews of *Jonah's Gourd Vine* took note of Hurston's substantial ability as a storyteller, her attention to intra-racial color prejudice and a skewed socio-economic system, her use of folklore and the southern black rural vernacular, and her unusual candor in revealing elements of black life. For today's readers, most contemporaneous reviews of Hurston's work reveal more about the ideological biases and critical limitations of the reviewers than they do about the quality and substance of Hurston's first novel.

In a July 11, 1934 review in *The New Republic*, Martha Gruening delighted in Hurston's revelations about the intimate life of "the Negro." Her excitement was echoed in Margaret Wallace's *New York Times* review on May 6, 1934. However, Estelle Fulton's August 1934 review in the Urban League magazine *Opportunity* found Hurston's novel lacking on several counts, including what she felt was the author's tendency to draw caricatures rather than real black people. Fulton nevertheless credited Hurston's "effective use of dialogue and traditional customs."[5] Andrew Burris's review in *The Crisis* concluded that the novel, despite its endorsements from "such eminent literary connoisseurs as Carl Van Vechten, Fannie Hust [sic], and Blanche Colton Williams," was "quite disappointing and a failure as a novel." Similarly to Fulton, Burris credited Hurston with having "captured the lusciousness and beauty of the Negro dialect as have few others," and this factor in combination with her rich display of folklore bestowed on the novel "an earthiness, a distinctly racial flavor; a somewhat primitive beauty which makes its defects the more regrettable." A dissenting opinion, published alongside Burris's decidedly negative review, pointed out that the success of Hurston's novel was evident in Burris's own praise for Hurston's successful use of folklore and black southern rural speech to shape an authentic tale. Indeed, in an April 18, 1934 letter to Eslanda Robeson (wife of Paul Robeson), Hurston wrote that several members of the Harlem literati had one night argued with her that "folk sources were no[t] important, nobody was interested, waste of time, it wasnt [sic] art nor even necessary thereto, ought to be suppressed, etc. etc., but I stuck to my guns and the world is certainly coming my way in regards to the Negro." Hurston insisted that the representation of authentic black life such as that presented in *Jonah's Gourd Vine* would supplant the inferior and synthetic minstrel tradition.[6] Josephine Pinckney's May 6, 1934 review of the novel in the *New York Herald Tribune Books* was generally positive and reflected a deeper critical engagement. Pinckney recognized Hurston's substantial talent and offered the following assessment:

> This novel of Negro life is the product of a fortunate combination of circumstances. The author writes as a Negro understanding her people and having opportunities that could come to no white person, however sympathetic, of seeing them when they are utterly themselves. But she

writes as a Negro whose intelligence is firmly in the saddle, who recognizes the value of an objective style in writing, and who is able to use the wealth of material available to her with detachment and with a full grasp of its dramatic qualities. Considering her especial temptations, her sustaining of the objective viewpoint is remarkable.[7]

Pinckney, in effect, praises Hurston for her ability to stress the importance of individual responsibility even during the worst of American social and political times for African Americans. And, yet, we find in Pinckney's praise some of the same ideological biases and limited vision of other contemporaneous reviewers, regardless of race.

As Hurston's first effort, *Jonah's Gourd Vine* is far from perfect; however, since Hurston's literary resurrection, critics have found much that is worthy of serious scholarly inquiry in all of Hurston's works. In her 2005 study of Hurston and southern literary culture, M. Genevieve West considers the above reviews and others (including reviews by Sterling Brown and Alain Locke); she notes the obvious: because contemporaneous critics could not read the novel alongside Hurston's entire corpus, they simply could not speak with any real knowledge of the author's agenda. West's conclusion that the novel is "cleverly subversive" is an understatement. Eric Sundquist describes *Jonah's Gourd Vine* as "a palimpsest of autobiographical and cultural rumination that not only fuses her [Hurston's] family history to fieldwork and theory but, in fact, self-consciously extends the attack on the boundary between ethnology and narrative that she had begun in *Mules and Men*, which was written before but published after *Jonah's Gourd Vine*." Karla Holloway reveals the value of Hurston's work to the field of Linguistics in her semiological analyses of Hurston's novels. Of *Jonah's Gourd Vine*, she argues that neither characters nor events "have power equal to the word," and that the novel "gathers its massive strength" from its "magical words."[8] Susan Edwards Meisenhelder's "'Natural Men' and 'Pagan Poesy' in *Jonah's Gourd Vine*" explores racial and gender dynamics in Hurston's representation of black manhood, and John Lowe examines the novel's "sorrowful humor" in his highly insightful *Jump at the Sun: Zora Neale Hurston's Cosmic Comedy* (1997). Finally, poet Rita Dove, in her foreword to the 1990 Harper Perennial edition of *Jonah's Gourd Vine*, finds much to recommend. Despite the novel's flaws, Dove notes, "Hurston's language is superb," and her omniscient narrator "neither indulges nor condemns the actions of her characters but offers the complexity of life in a story that leaves judgment up to the reader." Dove picks up on a significant aspect of Hurston's overall strategy as a black woman writer whose work was subject to the scrutiny and editing of a white male-dominated publishing industry trying to please a predominantly white readership. Dove continues, noting that Hurston presents protagonist

John Pearson "as a human being in all his individual paradoxes – troubled and gifted, dignified and lascivious, pure and selfish – and as the exemplification of the country preacher, he is both poet and philosopher."[9] In short, Hurston exhibits, even in her earliest work of long fiction, much of the skill that one finds in some of America's most accomplished authors.

## *Mules and Men* (1935)

Brisk sales of Hurston's first collection of folk tales no doubt benefited from the fact that famous Columbia University anthropologist Franz Boas wrote the preface for the volume, and the dust jacket featured an endorsement by the equally famous anthropologist Melville Herskovits. Celebrated poet Carl Sandburg weighed in with high praise for Hurston's achievement, though some critics questioned the author's aesthetic choice to diverge from the usual dry, scientific mode by inserting a narrator who sets up the tales in terms of context, performance, and function – a choice that worked especially well for Hurston.

As with *Jonah's Gourd Vine*, reviews of *Mules and Men* were often split along racial lines. While a number of white critics praised Hurston for her objectivity in presenting authentic "Negro" life, others used her work to affirm their own ideological biases. For example, David Cohn used Hurston's work to support his ideological predisposition that blacks are inherently violent and intellectually inferior. Often white reviewers praised the work for being an entertaining, authentic, and quaintly picaresque incursion into black southern rural life. White critics in general preferred the folk tales over the section on Voodoo. Lewis Gannett wrote in *The New York Herald Tribune Weekly Book Review* that he could not "remember anything better since *Uncle Remus*." Uncle Remus was the title character, narrator, and "happy darky" figure of Joel Chandler Harris's adapted and compiled folk tales taken from African American life. To compare Hurston's work to Harris's work is to compare the indigenous person's knowledge of local custom to that of the missionary. Nevertheless, Gannett took his cue from Boas's preface in making the comparison. Interestingly, Hurston wrote a gushing letter of thanks to Gannett describing his criticism as "so full of understanding kindness."[10]

The paternalistic tone of H. I. Brock's November 10, 1935 *New York Times Book Review* article is all too apparent: "a young Negro woman with a college education has invited the outside world to listen in while her own people are being as natural as they can never be when white folks are literally present . . . when Negroes are having a good gregarious time, dancing, singing, fishing, and . . . incessantly, talking." Brock's tone continues throughout his hearty and enthusiastic recommendation of Hurston's work. His favorite part of the work, he notes, is the "collection of competitive 'lies' from the treasurey [sic] of Afro-American folklore." Samuel Gaillard Stoney (*New York Herald Tribune*) and Jonathan Daniels (*The Saturday Review*) applauded the collection as "an excellent piece of reporting."[11] The *New Republic*'s Henry Lee Moon pronounced the volume "more than a collection of folklore" and added that it offered a "valuable picture of the life of the unsophisticated Negro in the small towns and backwoods of Florida."[12]

Among most black critics and some left-leaning white critics, the consensus was that Hurston was at best an accommodationist and at worst an opportunist and a sellout. African American critics Alain Locke and Sterling Brown wrote reviews that responded to comparisons between Hurston's work and that of Joel Chandler Harris, and also to white critics' tendencies to celebrate what they saw as Hurston's authenticity and objectivity. Locke and Brown were concerned that Hurston's work distorted African American realities. For Locke, the concern was that her work confirmed racial stereotypes and undermined attempts by black America to expose the harsh realities of Jim Crow living. Brown felt that Hurston's work lacked an element of bitterness that would make it more authentic. B. C. McNeill wrote in the *Journal of Negro History* that Hurston's style of presenting folk tales was unique and seemed to indicate that she was more of a novelist than a cultural historian. The contemporaneous consensus among white critics – with some notable exceptions in Harold Preece and C. Leslie Frazier, who wrote pointedly that Hurston lacked objectivity and wrote with a white audience in mind – was that the collection was revelatory and entertaining. Still, even Hurston's worst critics were forced to admit that she had accomplished in her writing a rare intimacy with the objects of her study, an intimacy and mode of mediation that gave her work the uniqueness for which it is today applauded.

Recent critical work on *Mules and Men* benefits from expanded knowledge of Hurston's own expository writings and her philosophy in general. Lippincott's marketing of the volume did nothing to help dissuade racialized responses to the text. In her excellent contextual analyses of Hurston's critical reception, M. Genevieve West notes that while the cover image of the 1942 volume is benign enough, the language used inside the dust jacket has a different effect. The language describes *Mules and Men* as "One of the most complete collections of American negro folklore that has ever been published," which includes "authentic descriptions of the weird hoodoo practices carried on by negroes in the South today." As West points out, the two statements "engage entirely different discourses. The first suggests that the volume represents a scientific achievement," and the second simultaneously speaks to the collection's authenticity while "dismissing it as less-than-serious-scholarship."[13] Finally, the fact that Hurston was operating in a public sphere dominated by men must always be taken into consideration.

Since Hurston's literary resurrection, critics have found *Mules and Men* to be – among other things – a subversively womanist text, an amazing testament of black people's sensual engagement with language, and a landmark ethnographic study of southern culture that charted new terrain in anthropological procedure. Perhaps most significantly, critics note Hurston's engagement with and celebration of West African ways of being in relating the folk tales and religious practices. In a 1989 essay, Cheryl Wall referred to *Mules and Men* as "a widely recognized if under discussed classic in Afro-American literature and American anthropology." More importantly, she noted how the title masks the volume's celebration of women, allowing Hurston to critique enforced gender roles just as she had done in previous works, including *Jonah's Gourd Vine*.[14] Wall notes, along with Susan Edwards Meisenhelder and others, Hurston's subversive agenda of liberating the black woman's voice in *Mules and Men*. Feminist and womanist readings of Hurston's entire corpus reveal her enduring engagement with this agenda, which is particularly evident in *Their Eyes Were Watching God*.

## Their Eyes Were Watching God (1937)

J. B. Lippincott released Hurston's second novel when the urban social protest novel was in vogue. *Their Eyes Were Watching God* did not fit the bill, and while this factor alone accounts for part of the novel's poor reception among contemporaneous critics, it certainly does not account for all of it. Once again, the black literary establishment largely panned the novel (and Hurston) for many of the very characteristics that bring it praise from contemporary critics. Sterling Brown – while noting that the novel revealed some bitterness (however obliquely) in its references to Nanny's sexual exploitation and ill treatment, and in the enforcement of Jim Crow rule in dealing with the dead following the hurricane – wondered where Hurston had hidden the ugliness of migrant work. (*Oprah Winfrey Presents Their Eyes Were Watching God*, a 2005 film adaptation of the novel, followed the novel in this regard.) Brown (who was adept at capturing folk speech in his poetry) directed his one note of praise to Hurston's capacity for recording and creating folk speech: "Her devotion to these people has rewarded her; *Their Eyes Were Watching God* is chockfull of earthy and touching poetry." Alain Locke suggested that *Their Eyes Were Watching God* represented an oversimplification of black life, and Ralph Ellison questioned Hurston's authorial integrity while characterizing her work as cal-culated burlesque;[15] in the latter characterization, Ellison seems particularly apt, for Hurston is clearly engaged in a distortion that aims to both reveal and conceal simultaneously. Such maneuverings are present in most of her work, requiring the reader to consume each layer carefully lest they mistake Hurston's rich meal for an unsatisfying light snack.

Witness Richard Wright's *New Masses* review dated October 5, 1937; Wright, who would soon publish the American classic *Native Son* (1940), stopped just short of referring to Hurston as an *Uncle Tom*. Unlike Sterling Brown, Wright had no appreciation for dialect and instead characterized her prose as being "cloaked in that facile sensuality that has dogged Negro expression since the days of Phillis Wheatley." He sees her carrying on in the tradition of minstrelsy: "The sensory sweep of her novel carries no theme, no message, no thought. In the main, her novel is not addressed to the Negro, but to a white audience whose chauvinistic tastes she knows how to satisfy. She exploits the phase of Negro life which is 'quaint,' the phase which evokes a piteous smile on the lips of the "superior" race."[16] His own inferiority complex showing, Wright displayed his bias toward social protest literature and his desire to set rigid parameters for Hurston's creative work. His assessment of white responses to Hurston's work was, however, not altogether without merit.

White critic Lucille Tompkins described *Their Eyes Were Watching God* as "beautiful," its dialect "very easy to follow, and the images it carries . . . irre-sistible" (Gates and Appiah, *Zora Neale Hurston*, pp. 18–19). Tompkins saw in the novel a universal tale: "It is about Negroes . . . but really it is about every one, or least every one who isn't so civilized that he has lost the capacity for glory." In 2005, advertisements for *Oprah Winfrey Presents Their Eyes Were Watching God* also represented Janie Crawford's story as "universal," echoing Hurston's sentiments in "What White Publishers Won't Print." Hurston felt that one way to improve race relations was to show the commonality of our human expe-riences. The major accomplishment for *Their Eyes Were Watching God* in this regard is that she was able to do this while telling a highly specific story. Sheila Hibben noted that Hurston was someone who wrote "with her head as well as with her heart." Hibben characterized the novel as "sensitive," and "filled with the ache of her [Hurston's] own people." *The New Republic*'s Otis Fergu-son began his review thus: "It isn't that this novel is bad, but that it deserves to be better." Clearly uncomfortable with Hurston's "spoken word" style of writing, Ferguson felt the novel was filled with "overliterary expression" – too much prose – though he (somewhat ironically) expressed his pleasure that it depicted "Negro life in its naturally creative and unselfconscious grace." In contrast Ethel A. Forrest's review in *Journal of Negro History* praised Hurston's writing style as "natural and easy"; she felt the author deserved "great praise" for her "skill and effectiveness" in writing the novel. Forrest's insight was sufficiently prescient to suggest that *Their Eyes Were Watching God* was "in many respects an historical novel."[17] None of the critics knew, of course, that the novel was Hurston's homage to the love of her life.

Most early reviewers of *Their Eyes Were Watching God* clearly lacked the insight that historical distance, social innovation, and great strides in literary criticism and theory have brought to contemporary criticism of her work. Since Alice Walker's literary resurrection and Robert Hemenway's literary biography of Hurston, *Their Eyes Were Watching God* has been the subject of numerous books, essays, theses, and dissertations. Now considered a classic text in American and African American literature, it has been hailed as a heroic quest narrative, a black woman's *Künstlerroman*, and a neo-freedom narrative. It has been compared to canonical texts such as James Joyce's *A Portrait of the Artist as a Young Man* (1916) and Ralph Ellison's *Invisible Man* (1952), and deemed therefore worthy of closer scrutiny by members of the American literary establishment. Harold Bloom, for example, has decided that Hurston's work belongs to the heroic-vitalist tradition in English and American literature alongside works by (white male writers) Samuel Richardson, D. H. Lawrence, and Theodore Dreiser. Many of the best-known and most esteemed critics and theorists of African American and American literature have subjected the novel, which Hurston wrote in only seven weeks, to their most intense scrutiny.

Janie Mae Crawford Killicks Starks Woods has been hailed as Blues singer extraordinaire, whose story represents a history of black women in America from Nanny's time in slavery to Janie's psychic liberation during the Jim Crow era. Womanist and feminist analyses note Janie's journey toward self-actualization, from silence to voice. In the American literary canon, *Their Eyes Were Watching God* exemplifies the value of folklore, celebrating at an organic level the tradition of African American literature that began with oral forms brought from Africa and shaped to fit New World experiences. *Their Eyes Were Watching God* was immensely popular throughout the 1980s and 1990s as a subject for scholarly criticism and college courses that fell under several headings, including History, Literature, Women's Studies, and Anthropology. Scholars note the manner in which the novel disrupts and enhances literary canons and the way it celebrates an aesthetic that is distinctly African American.

## *Tell My Horse* (1938)

Contemporaneous reviews of *Tell My Horse* were mixed, and the volume sold poorly. Carter G. Woodson noted in the *Journal of Negro History* that the collection revealed that Hurston was more anthropologist than novelist. He added that it was "entertaining and at the same time one of value which scholars must take into consideration in the study of the Negro in the Western Hemisphere." Elmer Davis's October 15, 1938 *Saturday Review* article referenced Hurston's concern with the plight of Haitian women and her love of Haiti; Davis felt, however, that Hurston had not fully digested her material before publishing it.[18] Other critics agreed that the material lacked organization and required more explanation and analysis than Hurston provided. Still Carl Carmer's *New York Herald Tribune* review lauded Hurston for this latest effort: "Zora Hurston has come back from her visit to the two near islands with a harvest unbelievably rich . . . The judges who select the recipients of Guggenheim fellowships honored themselves and the purpose of the foundation they serve when they subsidized Zora Hurston's visit to Haiti. I hope the American reading public will encourage her further wanderings." M. Genevieve West offers the most comprehensive treatment of contexts for publication of Hurston's second collection of folklore, with special attention to Lippincott's racially chauvinist marketing strategies. West points out that even before the volume appeared, it had generated angry protest against Hurston for her treatment of the untutored and illiterate. Julia E. R. Clark, writing from Haiti after hearing of comments Hurston made at two New York lectures on the subject of her recent research in Jamaica and Haiti, asserted that Hurston's "superficial study" represented a form of "impertinence."[19] *Tell My Horse* was subsequently published as *Voodoo Gods: An Inquiry into Native Myths and Magic in Jamaica and Haiti* (1939) in Great Britain, where it was much better received.

Harper & Row's 1990 edition of *Tell My Horse* contains a glowing recommendation from novelist and critic Ishmael Reed. A neo-Hoodoo aestheticist, Reed calls the collection a "major work of the Voodoo bibliography . . . a treasure for the English reader who is curious about the subject," and a "pioneer work." Reed felt that Hurston's "greatest accomplishment" in *Tell My Horse* was "in revealing the profound beauty and appeal of a faith older than Christianity, Buddhism, and Islam, a faith that has survived in spite of its horrendously bad reputation and the persecution of its followers."[20] While his prediction that the volume would become "the postmodernist book of the nineties" has thus far proven to be something of an overstatement, *Tell My Horse* has – for the past two decades – been read through a variety of lenses (including postmodernism) in such essays as Pamela Glenn Menke's "'The Lips of Books': Hurston's *Tell My Horse* and *Their Eyes Were Watching God* as Metalingual Texts," Amy Fass Emery's "The Zombie In/As the Text: Zora Neale Hurston's *Tell My Horse*," Annette Trefzer's "Possessing the Self: Caribbean Identities in Zora Neale Hurston's *Tell My Horse*," and John Carlos Rowe's "Opening the Gate to the Other America: The Afro-Caribbean Politics of Zora Neale

Hurston's *Mules and Men* and *Tell My Horse*." In *The Character of the Word*, Karla Holloway points to the value of *Tell My Horse* in its anticipation of "black nationalism some thirty years before it found its way to the Americas,"[21] and in *Ethnic Modernisms: Anzia Yezierska, Zora Neale Hurston, Jean Rhys, and the Aesthetics of Dislocation*, Delia Caparoso Konzett examines the collection's transnational perspective on the African Diaspora. In addition to Harper's 1990 re-issue of *Tell My Horse*, Cheryl Wall included the collection in her 1995 edited volume for the Library of America, *Zora Neale Hurston: Folklore, Memoirs, & Other Writings*, providing a prestigious resource for scholars interested in Hurston's less-examined works. These new editions of Hurston's pioneering work in Caribbean folklore and Voodoo remain in print and thus are available for new and innovative scholarly inquiries. The research Hurston conducted for *Mules and Men* and *Tell My Horse* helped her to complete her next novel, which depicted the biblical Moses as the ultimate Hoodoo/Voodoo doctor.

## *Moses, Man of the Mountain* (1939)

Early reviews of Hurston's *Mules and Men* reflect problems of readership similar to those associated with her previous works. Critics could not and did not appreciate the complexity of Hurston's project of representing the folk figure Moses as transcending the Judeo-Christian tradition and, simultaneously, revealing the problems inherent to the tradition's patriarchal foundations. Alain Locke issued an unfavorable review in *Opportunity* magazine, and even Hurston expressed disappointment with the novel in letters to Edwin Osgood Grover and Carl Van Vechten.[22] In his November 11, 1939 *Saturday Review* article, Louis Untermeyer, who had written a biography of the biblical Moses, found the novel "as arresting as it is fresh," but felt its whole was "less successful than the parts . . . the total effect that of unfulfilled expectation." Still Untermeyer concluded that the work had "a racial vitality, a dramatic intensity worthy of its gifted author." Philip Slomovitz, writing for *Christian Century* on December 6, 1939, took issue with Hurston's depiction of Moses' ethical contributions but concluded that Hurston had "written a splendid study of slave emancipation," and "her biography of Moses is invaluable." Carl Carmer's *New York Herald Tribune* review concluded essentially that Hurston had written "a fine Negro novel." Percy Hutchinson's November 19, 1939 *New York Times Book Review* article, while racially condescending in tone, praised the novel as an "exceptionally fine piece of work far off the beaten tracks of literature," and "literature in every best sense of the word."[23] Hutchinson was most attracted to the quaint, colorful, homespun depictions of the intimate lives of black Americans. While

Hutchinson saw Hurston's break with literary tradition as a plus, Ralph Ellison felt the novel did nothing to advance the cause of black fiction and saw Hurston's tendency to chart her own path and ignore literary predecessors as a liability. Though Ellison would soon be at odds with Richard Wright over Wright's insistence on social protest literature, both writers were somewhat prescriptive and chauvinistic in their critiques of Hurston's work.

Some critics simply did not know what to make of the novel. Robert Bone actually characterized it as folklore in his *The Negro Novel in America* (1958); however, Blyden Jackson's 1953 article, "Some Negroes in the Land of Goshen," provided an insightful and intelligent assessment of the work. In 1971, Darwin Turner offered qualified praise for *Moses, Man of the Mountain* in an otherwise negative assessment of Hurston's literary career. Once again it was Blyden Jackson, in his introduction to the 1984 edition of *Moses, Man of the Mountain*, who saw a remarkable achievement in the novel: "In *Moses* Hurston rises to an occasion decidedly rare in Afro-American literature and even rarer in the national literature of which Afro-American literature is an integral part. If *Moses* is not Hurston's most acclaimed novel, it certainly should not be overlooked. It is protest that is, beautifully, all the better protest for the protest it is not."[24] More recent and in-depth critical attention to *Moses, Man of the Mountain* includes Karla Holloway's linguistic analysis in *The Character of the Word* (1987), John Lowe's "Signifying on God: *Moses, Man of the Mountain*," in *Jump at the Sun: Zora Neale Hurston's Cosmic Humor* (1997), Timothy P. Caron's chapter on the novel in *Race and Religion in O'Connor, Faulkner, Hurston, and Wright* (2000), Melanie Wright's chapter in *Moses in America: The Cultural Uses of Biblical Narrative* (2003), and Mark Christian Thompson's "National Socialism and Blood Sacrifice in Zora Neale Hurston's *Moses, Man of the Mountain*" (2004).

In her introduction to *Critical Essays on Zora Neale Hurston* (1998), Gloria Cronin described *Moses, Man of the Mountain* as "Hurston's assessment of 5,000 years of Judeo-Christian patriarchy, as manifested in Hitler's anti-Semitism and in American racism. Using a traditional reading of *Exodus* as a liberation story interpreted in the context of Black America, Hurston set about disclosing the deleterious effects on women and men of a Judeo-Christianity founded on the ideologies of the hypermasculine nation-state building."[25] The amount of serious scholarly inquiry being conducted on this and other Hurston works continues the project begun by Alice Walker and Robert Hemenway in the 1970s to rescue Hurston from her literary grave. Studies by John Lowe, Deborah Plant, and Susan Meisenhelder illuminate Hurston's success in blending allegory, humor, parody, and satire in her treatment of the race, class, and gender dynamics in African American life and culture in *Moses, Man of the Mountain*. Clearly, critics have taken note of the novel's complexity, assuring it a place in the academic universe. Biographer Valerie Boyd calls the novel a "tour de force of language, humor, insight, protest, and prophecy," blaming the flaws in the novel on Bertram Lippincott's conviction that Hurston's writing needed little or no editing – which is interesting considering the amount of editorial control Lippincott would exert on Hurston's autobiography.[26]

## *Dust Tracks on a Road* (1942)

When Hurston's *Dust Tracks on a Road* appeared in 1942, radical white reviewer Harold Preece called it "the tragedy of a gifted, sensitive mind, eaten up by an egocentrism fed on the patronizing admiration of the dominant white world." Black author and critic Arna Bontemps wrote sardonically that, "Miss Hurston deals very simply with the more serious aspects of Negro life in America – she ignores them."[27] These harsh reviews notwithstanding, *Dust Tracks on a Road* was Hurston's most successful volume to date. Sales were generally good. Reviews by white critics were overwhelmingly positive, the severely edited volume having resulted in a work that seemed to deny the existence of racism in America and so muted the author's incisive intellect and political consciousness that it had the effect of purging feelings of "white guilt," validating white apathy to racial oppression, and leaving many white readers feeling "warm and fuzzy." Though Phil Strong attempted to praise the work, his praise comes across in racist terms; Hurston's story, he writes, is "told in exactly the right manner, simply and with candor, with a seasoning – not overdone – of the marvelous locutions of the imaginative field nigger." He appreciated what he saw as Hurston's "lack of race-consciousness" and concluded that it was a "fine, rich autobiography, and heartening to anyone, white, black, or tan." Other highly favorable reviews appeared in the *New Yorker*, the *Pittsburgh Courier*, and *The New York Times*, where John Chamberlain described the volume as being "as beautiful as Cape jasmine – and as vulgar as a well-liquored fish fry." Writing for *The New York Times Book Review*, Beatrice Sherman stops just short of declaring Hurston a credit to her race. Unwittingly arrogant, she writes: "Then impression simmers down to a feeling that the author regards the Negro race much as she regards any other race – as made up of some good, some bad, and a lot of medium. The problems they face are those of any other race, with the disadvantage of being a *younger* lot. . . . Any race might well be proud to have more members of the caliber and stamina of Zora Neale Hurston" [my emphasis].[28] While Sherman's nod to Hurston for telling a story that transcends racial categories speaks to Hurston's own authorial desires, much of her assessment reveals a mindset tinged with a paternalist racial superiority complex.

While he had several negative criticisms of the volume that prevented his recommending it as "great autobiography," and he felt the work not completely truthful, Howard University professor W. Edward Farrison, felt he could nevertheless recommend it as worthwhile reading. Hazel Griggs called *Dust Tracks on a Road* a "brilliant and analytical portrait."[29] For many in the black literary establishment, however, *Dust Tracks on a Road* merely confirmed what they already suspected: that Hurston would do anything to get into print. While a few critics took note of the complex manner in which Hurston chose to relate her life story, others panned the award-winning work for a perceived host of sins. Thus, while she was hailed as a resounding success on the one hand – having won the Anisfeld Award in Race Relations and thus being sought out as a public speaker – she was considered by others to be a sellout and, for some (like Harold Preece), even worse.

Contemporary research into the production background of *Dust Tracks on a Road* has enhanced the critical terrain for reading and assessing the work. In all, four previously excised or greatly revised and reapportioned chapters have been restored to contemporary editions. Most readers today are much more likely to encounter a version of *Dust Tracks on a Road* with the excised sections restored. Cheryl Wall's "Notes on the Texts," included in her edited collection of Hurston's writings, Claudine Raynaud's "'Rubbing a Paragraph with a Soft Cloth': Muted Voices and Editorial Constraints in *Dust Tracks on a Road*" (1992), and "Autobiography as a Lying Session" (1998)[30] illustrate the impact of Hurston's Lippincott editors on her autobiography. Lippincott excised entire sections of *Dust Tracks on a Road*, sections which reflected Hurston's views on race, sexuality, and politics. In particular, Lippincott excised a chapter titled "The Inside Light – Being a Salute to Friendship," in which Hurston acknowledged people who had helped her along the way. The chapter would have served to counter the impression that she somehow made it on her own. In another excised chapter, "Seeing the World as It Is," Hurston had expressed her views on religion and socio-political matters, including the frank (and perhaps dangerous) admission that communism had its benefits but she lacked the herd mentality required to become one of the *flock*. She argued against the idea of a black monolith and also derided whites for feeling superior to others merely because they were white. Thus, several questions arise: Would the critical reception have been reversed (based on the critic's race) if Hurston had been allowed to tell her story her way in her own words? How might white reviewers respond to the knowledge that Hurston had indeed experienced racism on numerous occasions in democratic America? How would they have responded to her discussion of their false sense of superiority? How might they have responded to those excised sections of *Dust Tracks on a Road* in which she criticized the

United States for its part in global colonialism and imperialism? Would black reviewers and leftist white reviewers have been friendlier in their assessments, or had they already made up their minds about Hurston?

Even without the restored text and knowledge of the excessive editing that marked the 1942 edition of *Dust Tracks on a Road*, recent poststructuralist approaches to literary study allow for more complex analyses of Hurston's project than those performed by her contemporaneous critics. Critics studying the work since the 1980s understand that in order for Hurston to maneuver around Lippincott's conditions for production and publication, she had to engage her own folk wisdom and 'hit a straight lick with a crooked stick'. She had to do what Harriet Jacobs did in the early 1800s – make the best of a bad situation. Ultimately, the identity of the seemingly muted black woman emerging from Hurston's struggle to produce a volume appropriately representing her best self within the parameters of a racist, sexist, classist order serves as its own record, its own evidence. New scholarship on *Dust Tracks on a Road* proceeds with this knowledge and continues to mark the volume's value, depth, and dimension as an extraordinary work of American literature and a major contribution to women's autobiography.

## Seraph on the Suwanee (1948)

Hurston's final published novel was (at first) largely ignored by black reviewers for obvious reasons: not only did the literature deviate substantially from the protest aesthetic that reached its heyday in the 1940s but it also dealt only peripherally with black people – and (at least on the surface) in a not very constructive or positive manner. A few white critics were mildly unnerved by Hurston's depiction of poor southern whites and their southern rural dialects. Quaint and picaresque black folk depicted by a black author was one thing; quaint and picaresque white folk depicted by a black author was quite another. Still, the novel was generally well-received by white critics and became Hurston's best-selling work. Frank G. Slaughter, writing for the *New York Times Book Review*, credited Hurston with knowing "the Florida cracker of the swamps and turpentine camps intimately." He concluded that the novel gave the impression Hurston had taken a "textbook on Freudian psychology and adapted it to her needs, perhaps with her tongue in her cheek while so doing. The result is a curious mixture of excellent background drawing against which move a group of half-human puppets."[31] Slaughter's reference to Freudian psychoanalysis is related to the mental state of the novel's protagonist for most of the story. Worth Tuttle Hedden, writing for *the New York Herald Tribune*

*Books*, likewise found the novel "astonishing" and unique, though not perfect: "Reading this astonishing novel, you wish that Miss Hurston had used the scissors and smoothed the seams. Having read it, you would like to be able to remember every extraneous incident and every picaresque metaphor." For Hedden, the novel was rife with contradiction but nevertheless compelling. Hedden's comments should alert the contemporary reader to the fact of Hurston's multi-layered narrative; buried inside the too-dense narrative (which perhaps reminds contemporary critics of a plodding James Baldwin novel) are numerous folk wisdoms, narratives of race and gender, and a blueprint for the American success story. Hurston's associate Carl Van Vechten described the novel as superb, and Harnett T. Kane felt Hurston "caught so magnificently the speech, the movement, the nuances of thought among the *lesser* whites" (my emphasis).[32] Three thousand copies of the novel sold within the first few days of release and a second printing of 2,000 copies was ordered.

Hurston would not enjoy the novel's popularity for long however, because false felony charges of child molestation were filed against her soon after the book's release and the black press took especial note; the Baltimore-based *Afro-American* published a sensationalized story about the charges, designed to hurt Hurston as much as possible. The *Afro-American* headline and subheading read: "Novelist Arrested in Morals Charge," "Review of Author's Latest Book Notes Character Is 'Hungry for Love.'" Continuing with language from the novel, the writer added the attention-grabbing question: "Did She Want 'Knowing and Doing' Kind of Love?"[33] Language used to express the desires between the married couple at the center of the novel, Jim and Arvay Meserve, had been taken out of context to insinuate that Hurston was the kind of libido-driven person who lusted after and molested young retarded boys. The article included a highly unflattering photo of Hurston to reinforce the insinuation. The story was picked up and carried by other newspapers around the country, and what bothered Hurston most about the incident was that she had been so brutally and gleefully betrayed by another black person: the black court employer who took the story to the press. The affair caused Zora to cease promotional activities associated with her new novel and leave Harlem. She even contemplated suicide. That same winter, she found herself defending other false charges in small claims court. Her legal fees ate up the royalties from *Seraph on the Suwanee* and, desperate for money but afraid to venture out to work, she was forced to borrow money from friends.

Hurston biographer Robert Hemenway says of Hurston's decision to write *Seraph on the Suwanee* that she "largely turned her back on the source of her creativity," clearly suggesting that the novel lacks merit because it does not derive from organic black experience. Searching for an explanation for the novel, Hemenway points to biographical evidence that "Hurston was groping toward a statement about marriage." Hemenway seems to wax conservative in his suggestion that Hurston's "relatively liberated" attitudes about her personal heterosexual relationships, her preference for temporary liaisons, informed her objectives in *Seraph on the Suwanee*. Yet, he concludes that ultimately *Seraph on the Suwanee* fails as a novel because Hurston is unable to move her protagonist "'from fear into self-confidence'"; she could not "grant Arvay the attainment of a truly independent selfhood, the kind that Zora Neale Hurston had established in her own life." Hemingway fails to see Arvay's transformation from passive acquiescence to active acceptance of her role as Jim Meserve's partner. To be sure, Arvay Henson is no Zora Neale Hurston, and certainly she is no model of twentieth-century feminist consciousness. Writing within the constraints of the postwar promotion of domestic bliss, Hurston chose the path of least resistance in her subversive rendering of the marital relationship. In the end, Jim depends on Arvay's nurturing more than she depends on his maleness. Psychologically, she is the stronger of the two in the end, the self-reflexive and introspective member of the marriage. She is also a changed woman who chooses to be an active partner in her marriage. Hemenway and most other critics also miss Hurston's critique of the socio-economic order that privileges whiteness. Hemenway concludes that Hurston's "political opinions had fallen victim to publishers' demands."[34]

Contemporary scholars note Hurston's deft treatment of gender conventions in *Seraph on the Suwanee*. Susan Meisenhelder reads the metaphors in *Seraph on the Suwanee* against those of *Their Eyes Were Watching God* to reveal Hurston's critique of the dominant culture's "models of identity and relationships for black women and men." Arvay Meserve's position represents that of the protected white woman propped up on a pedestal – the position Nanny of *Their Eyes Were Watching God* desired for her granddaughter, Janie. Jim Meserve is the prototype for the big voice that Jody Starks does his best to emulate. Hurston takes the careful reader inside these two admired types and reveals their clay feet. As Meisenhelder points out, Hurston wrapped her critique "in the cloak of romance, a version of the 'poor girl marries rich boy' story she claimed was the favorite white theme, and by seeming to validate the traditional American values of hard work, tough men, and loyal women, Hurston hoped to write a popular novel, one that would be financially successful, marketed by book clubs, and made into a Hollywood film."[35] Similarly, Janet St. Clair, in "The Courageous Undertow of Zora Neale Hurston's *Seraph on the Suwanee*," argues that both Hurston and her *whiny* white protagonist, Arvay Meserve, have been too harshly judged by critics. St. Clair concludes that "although the weaknesses of the novel are real, the inconsistencies are the result of a subversive feminist substory that has so far gone unrecognized, a narrative of resistance and self-discovery that exists not between the lines but solidly on every page." St. Clair argues further that Arvay's "persistent attempts to preserve her integrity through withdrawal, resistance, and suspicion are motivated by a tenacious belief in her own intrinsic worth and in her rights to individual freedom and social respect. Because she is consistently denied access to the power of both word and deed, her progress is slow."[36] In short, though it was intended as a popular novel that would be a commercial success, *Seraph on the Suwanee* exemplifies the same density of Hurston's other works and is highly deserving of sustained critical attention.

*Seraph on the Suwanee* performed sufficiently well for Scribner's to prod Hurston on her next novel, "The Lives of Barney Turk," another story featuring primarily white characters which she worked on during 1949 but which Scribner's subsequently declined to publish. We can blame the unfortunate events occurring in the wake of *Seraph on the Suwanee's* publication in part for Hurston's literary decline in subsequent years. We can never know for certain how much her own (razors of personal) vanity and rugged individualism contributed to her dwindling literary and personal fortunes. Today, she is as much a part of the canons of African American literature and American literature as Nobel Laureate Toni Morrison.

## Notes

1. In Wall, *Folklore, Memoirs and Other Writings*, pp. 950–5; here pp. 952–3.
2. In Wall, *Folklore, Memoirs and Other Writings*, p. 827.
3. Richard Wright, "Between Laughter and Tears," October 1937, rpt. in *Critical Essays on Zora Neale Hurston*, ed. Gloria L. Cronin (New York: G. K. Hall, 1998), pp. 75–6; Langston Hughes, "The Negro Artist and the Racial Mountain," 1926, *The Norton Anthology of African American Literature*, ed. Henry Louis Gates *et al.* (New York: W. W. Norton, 1997), pp. 1267–71.
4. Wallace, in Henry Louis Gates and Kwame Anthony Appiah, eds., *Zora Neale Hurston: Critical Perspectives Past and Present* (New York: Amistad, 1987), pp. 8–9; Burris, in Cronin, *Critical Essays*, pp. 35–6.
5. Felton, in Gates and Appiah, *Zora Neale Hurston*, pp. 4–5; Burris, in Cronin, *Critical Essays*, p. 36.
6. In Kaplan, *Zora Neale Hurston*, p. 300.
7. Pinckney, in Cronin, *Critical Essays*, p. 33.
8. M. Genevieve West, *Zora Neale Hurston and American Literary Culture* (Gainesville, FL: University Press of Florida, 2005), p. 76; Sundquist, "'The Drum with the Man Skin' *Jonah's Gourd Vine*," in Gates and Appiah, *Zora Neale Hurston*, pp. 39–66,

p. 51; Karla Holloway, *The Character of the Word: The Texts of Zora Neale Hurston* (New York: Greenwood Press, 1987), p. 69.

9. Rita Dove, "Foreword," *JGV* (1934; New York: Harper Perennial, 1990), pp. vii–xv.

10. Gannett, in Gates and Appiah, *Zora Neale Hurston*, p. 11.

11. Brock, ibid, pp. 13–14; West, *Zora Neale Hurston*, p. 81.

12. Moon, in Gates and Appiah, *Zora Neale Hurston*, p. 10.

13. West, *Zora Neale Hurston* pp. 77–8.

14. Wall, "Mules and Men and Women," in Cronin, *Critical Essays*, pp. 53–70.

15. Brown, in Gates and Appiah, *Zora Neale Hurston*, pp. 20–1; Locke, ibid., p. 18; Ralph Ellison, "Recent Negro Fiction," *New Masses* 40.6 (August 5, 1941): 22–6.

16. Wright, in Gates and Appiah, *Zora Neale Hurston*, pp. 16–17; Tompkins, ibid., pp. 18–19.

17. Hibben, ibid., pp. 21–2; Ferguson, ibid., pp. 22–3; Ethel A. Forrest, Review of *Their Eyes Were Watching God, Journal of Negro History* 23.1 (January 1938): 106–7.

18. Carter G. Woodson, Review of *Tell My Horse, Journal of Negro History* 24 (January 1939): 116–18; Elmer Davis, Review of *Tell My Horse*, in Gates and Appiah, *Zora Neale Hurston*, pp. 24–5; Carl Carmer, "In Haiti and Jamaica," ibid., pp. 143–4.

19. Quoted in West, *Zora Neale Hurston*, p. 133.

20. Ishmael Reed, "Foreword," *TMH* (New York: Harper Perennial, 1995), pp. xi–xv.

21. Holloway, *The Character of the Word*, p. 110.

22. Kaplan, *Zora Neale Hurston*, pp. 422–4.

23. Untermeyer, in Gates and Appiah, *Zora Neale Hurston*, pp. 26–7; Slomovitz, in Cronin, *Critical Essays*, pp. 152–3; Carmer, "Biblical Story in Negro Rhythm," *New York Herald Tribune* (November 26, 1939): 5; Percy Hutchinson, in Gates and Appiah, *Zora Neale Hurston*, pp. 27–9.

24. Blyden Jackson, "Introduction," *Moses, Man of the Mountain* (Urbana and Chicago, IL: University of Illinois Press, 1984), pp. vi–xix.

25. Cronin *Critical Essays*, p. 13.

26. Boyd, *Wrapped in Rainbows*, p. 335.

27. Preece, quoted in West, *Zora Neale Hurston*, pp. 185–6; Arna Bontemps, "From Eatonville, Fla. To Harlem," *New York Herald Tribune Books* 22 (November 1942): 3.

28. Strong, in Cronin, *Critical Essays*, pp. 167–9; John Chamberlain, "Books of the Times," Review of *Dust Tracks on a Road, New York Times* 7 (November 1942): 13; Sherman, in Gates and Appiah, *Zora Neale Hurston*, pp. 32–3.

29. Farrison, quoted in West, *Zora Neale Hurston*, p. 184; Griggs, quoted in West, *Zora Neale Hurston*, p. 182.

30. " 'Rubbing a Paragraph with a Soft Cloth': Muted Voices and Editorial Constraints in *Dust Tracks on a Road*," in *De/Colonizing the Subject: The Politics of Gender in Women's Autobiography*, ed. Sidonie Smith and Julia Watson (Minneapolis, MN: University of Minnesota Press, 1992), pp. 35–64; "Autobiography as a Lying Session," in *Black Feminist Theory*, ed. Joe Weixlmann and Houston A. Baker (Greenwood, FL: Penkevill, 1998), pp. 111–38.

31. Slaughter, in Gates and Appiah, *Zora Neale Hurston*, pp. 34–5.
32. Hedden, ibid., pp. 35–6; quoted in West, *Zora Neale Hurston*, p. 215.
33. Quoted in Boyd, *Wrapped in Rainbows*, pp. 395–6.
34. Hemenway, *Zora Neale Hurston*, pp. 310–13.
35. Susan Edwards Meisenhelder, *Hitting a Straight Lick with a Crooked Stick: Race and Gender in the Work of Zora Neale Hurston* (Tuscaloosa, AL: University of Alabama Press, 1999), p. 92.
36. Janet St. Clair, "The Courageous Undertow of Zora Neale Hurston's *Seraph on the Suwanee*," *Modern Language Quarterly* 50.1 (March 1989): 38–57.

# Suggestions for further reading

Bloom, Harold, ed. *Zora Neale Hurston's Their Eyes Were Watching God*. Modern Critical Interpretations. Philadelphia, PA: Chelsea House Publishers, 1987. Bloom collects some of the best and most revelatory scholarship then available for Hurston's best-known novel. Contributors include Robert Stepto, Lorraine Bethel, Barbara Johnson, and Henry Louis Gates, Jr.

Bordelon, Pamela, ed. *Go Gator and Muddy the Water: Writings by Zora Neale Hurston from the Federal Writers' Project*. New York: W. W. Norton, 1999. The volume collects Hurston's work products and oral history materials from her Federal Writers' Project experiences during the 1930s; many of the materials are published here for the first time. They are particularly useful as source material for *Their Eyes Were Watching God*.

Boyd, Valerie. *Wrapped in Rainbows: The Life of Zora Neale Hurston*. New York: Scribner's, 2003. Boyd's work reigns as the most comprehensive assessment of the author's life.

Cronin, Gloria L., ed. *Critical Essays on Zora Neale Hurston*. New York: G. K. Hall & Co., 1998. The volume includes some contemporaneous reviews of Hurston's works that are not included in the earlier volume by Gates and Appiah (referenced below), along with several new essays. See especially the essays by Wall and St. Clair.

Davis, Rose Parkman. *Zora Neale Hurston: An Annotated Bibliography and Reference Guide*. Boston, MA: G. K. Hall, 1997. This volume's significance is made obvious by its title.

Gates, Henry Louis, and Kwame Anthony Appiah, eds. *Zora Neale Hurston: Critical Perspectives Past and Present*. New York: Amistad, 1987. The comprehensive nature of the volume is what made it unique in 1993. Gates and Appiah collected contemporaneous reviews and the best essays on Hurston available at the time. Readers should take special note of Françoise Lionnet-McCumber's essay on *Dust Tracks on a Road*.

Glassman, Steve, and Kathryn Lee Seidel, eds. *Zora in Florida*. Orlando, FL: University of Central Florida Press, 1991. The unique essays in this volume explore Florida as setting and backdrop for Hurston's life philosophy and literary works.

Harris, Trudier. *The Power of the Porch: The Storyteller's Craft in Zora Neale Hurston, Gloria Naylor, and Randall Kenan*. Athens, GA: University of Georgia Press, 1996. Harris's work explores storytelling in Hurston's *Mules and Men*, and connects her use of storytelling as narrative strategy to a rich tradition in African American life and culture.

Hemenway, Robert. *Zora Neale Hurston: A Literary Biography*. Chicago and Urbana, IL: University of Illinois Press, 1980. Until Valerie Boyd's 2003 biography of Hurston appeared, Hemenway's work was the first serious and most thorough treatment of Hurston's life and work.

Holloway, Karla. *The Character of the Word: The Texts of Zora Neale Hurston*. New York: Greenwood Press, 1987. Holloway explores Hurston's works through the lenses of formal Linguistics and African American spiritual traditions.

Howard, Lillie P., ed. *Alice Walker and Zora Neale Hurston: The Common Bond*. Westport, CT: Greenwood Press, 1993. Howard collects essays by Alice Walker, Trudier Harris, Ann Folwell Stanford, Ayana Karanja, and others. The volume's significance is apparent in its title; the essays examine intertextual and extratextual linkages between Hurston and Alice Walker, the woman who was instrumental in resurrecting Hurston as literary foremother for succeeding generations of African American women writers.

Hurston, Anne. *Speak, So You Can Speak Again: The Life of Zora Neale Hurston*. New York: Doubleday, 2004. A Hurston family descendant has compiled a unique collection of memorabilia that includes numerous photographs, replicas of handwritten notes, and other documents from the author's life that readers will find fascinating. The material is presented along with an intimate sketch of the author's personal life.

Hurston, Zora Neale. *Every Tongue Got to Confess: Negro Folk-Tales from the Gulf States*. Fwd. John Edgar Wideman; Introd. Carla Kaplan. New York: HarperCollins, 2001. The volume features folk tales from Hurston's field notes as she took them down while traveling through the south on an anthropology fellowship. It is a wonderful supplement to *Mules and Men*.

Kaplan, Carla, ed. *Zora Neale Hurston: A Life in Letters*. New York: Doubleday, 2002. Kaplan has collected letters Hurston wrote to her many friends and associates from the 1920s through the 1950s. In many cases, the letters provide insight into the motivations of a woman who often obscured her private self.

Lester, Neal A. *Understanding Zora Neale Hurston's Their Eyes Were Watching God: A Student Casebook to Issues, Sources, and Historical Documents*. Westport, CT: Greenwood Press, 1999. Lester's book provides useful and essential materials for a deeper contextual engagement with Hurston's most popular work.

Lowe, John. *Jump at the Sun: Zora Neale Hurston's Cosmic Comedy*. Chicago and
     Urbana, IL: University of Illinois Press, 1994. Lowe's seminal work
     showcases the function of humor in African American literature and
     culture generally and specifically in Hurston's longer fiction. Lowe's
     reading of *Seraph on the Suwanee* is particularly revealing in regard to
     Arvay Meserve's lack of "mother wit".
Meisenhelder, Susan Edwards. *Hitting a Straight Lick with a Crooked Stick: Race
     and Gender in the Work of Zora Neale Hurston*. Tuscaloosa, AL: University
     of Alabama Press, 1999. Using the folk euphemism for making the best
     of a bad situation as a rubric, Meisenhelder's work reveals the subversive
     nature of Hurston's literary projects and her objective of liberating
     women from patriarchal constraints and limited gender roles. Her
     reading of *Seraph on the Suwanee* is particularly valuable.
Peters, Pearlie. *The Assertive Woman in Zora Neale Hurston's Fiction, Folklore, and
     Drama*. New York: Routledge, 1998. The volume explores the evolution
     of the individualist spirit and the assertive woman's voice in Hurston's
     work. Significantly, Peters includes analyses of some of Hurston's
     seldom-assessed dramatic works.
Plant, Deborah G. *Every Tub Must Sit on Its Own Bottom: The Philosophy and
     Politics of Zora Neale Hurston*. Urbana and Chicago, IL: University of
     Illinois Press, 1995. The one volume devoted specifically and pointedly
     to Hurston's philosophy and politics. Using the folk euphemism for
     self-reliance and self-determination as a rubric, Plant connects
     Hurston's thinking to Nietzsche, Spinoza, Booker T. Washington, and
     others, which significantly aids our understanding of Hurston's politics,
     influences, and motivations.
—*Zora Neale Hurston: A Biography of the Spirit*. Westport, CT: Praeger, 2007.
     The most recent biography of Hurston examines the author's spiritual
     development and how it propelled her extraordinary life achievements.
Walker, Alice. *In Search of Our Mothers' Gardens: Womanist Prose*. New York:
     Harcourt Brace and Company, 1983. Walker details her role in
     resurrecting Hurston as a literary foremother. Walker was instrumental
     in moving Hurston to the center of the canon of African American
     women's literature.
Wall, Cheryl. *Women of the Harlem Renaissance*. Bloomington, IN: Indiana
     University Press, 1995. Wall uses the lenses of race and gender to offer an
     incisive assessment of Hurston's work alongside that of several of her
     contemporary women writers during the Harlem Renaissance.
—ed. *Their Eyes Were Watching God: A Casebook*, New York: Oxford University
     Press, 2000. Wall has collected essential readings for understanding
     Hurston's best-known work. Readers should note especially Daphne
     Lamothe's essay on Voodoo imagery in the novel.
West, M. Genevieve. *Zora Neale Hurston & American Literary Culture*. Gainesville,
     FL: University Press of Florida, 2005. The volume contains an incisive,

sustained, comprehensive analysis of circumstances contributing to contemporaneous receptions of each of Hurston's works.

Zora Neale Hurston annual festival site: http://www.zoranealehurstonfestival. com. The site contains information and photographs about Hurston, African American culture, and the annual Zora Neale Hurston festival in Eatonville, Florida.

# Index

# The Cambridge Introductions to . . .